Understanding Emotional

Rational emotive behaviour therapy (REBT) is an approach to counselling and psychotherapy rooted in the CBT tradition and one that has a distinctive perspective on emotional problems.

Understanding Emotional Problems provides an accurate understanding of the REBT perspective on eight major emotional problems for which help is sought:

- anxiety
- depression
- shame
- guilt
- unhealthy anger
- hurt
- unhealthy jealousy
- unhealthy envy.

Rather than discussing treatment methods, Windy Dryden encourages the reader to accurately understand these problems and suggests that a clear, correct understanding of each disorder will provide a firm foundation for effective treatment.

This concise, straightforward text presents each emotional problem in a similar way, allowing the reader to compare and contrast the similarities and differences between problems. *Understanding Emotional Problems* will be essential reading for therapists both in training and in practice.

Windy Dryden is Professor of Psychotherapeutic Studies at Goldsmiths College, London.

Understanding Emotional Problems

The REBT Perspective

Windy Dryden

Routledge
Taylor & Francis Group

LONDON AND NEW YORK

First published 2009 by Routledge
27 Church Road, Hove, East Sussex BN3 2FA

Simultaneously published in the USA and Canada
by Routledge
711 Third Avenue, New York, NY 10017, USA

Routledge is an imprint of the Taylor & Francis Group, an informa business

Typeset in Times by Garfield Morgan, Swansea, West Glamorgan
Cover design by Andy Ward

British Library Cataloguing in Publication Data
A catalogue record for this book is available from the British Library

Library of Congress Cataloging-in-Publication Data
Dryden, Windy.
    Understanding emotional problems : the REBT perspective / Windy
Dryden.
    p. ; cm.
    Includes bibliographical references and index.
    ISBN 978-0-415-48196-0 (hbk) – ISBN 978-0-415-48197-7 (pbk) 1.
Rational emotive behavior therapy. I. Title.
    [DNLM: 1. Psychotherapy, Rational-Emotive–methods. 2. Behavior
Therapy–methods. WM 420.5.P8 D799u 2009]
    RC489.R3D82 2009
    616.89'14–dc22

                                                    2008027772

ISBN: 978-0-415-48196-0 (hbk)
ISBN: 978-0-415-48197-7 (pbk)

Contents

Introduction

My purpose in this book is to outline the Rational Emotive Behaviour Therapy (REBT) perspective on the eight major emotional problems that people seek help for: anxiety, depression, shame, guilt, unhealthy anger, hurt, unhealthy jealousy and unhealthy envy. This will be a book on understanding these problems, not on how to treat them, for effective treatment needs to be based on an accurate understanding and this is what I aim to provide here.

While REBT is an approach to counselling and psychotherapy that is rooted firmly in the CBT tradition, it does have a distinctive perspective on emotional problems. As you will see from the following chapters, the REBT perspective argues that:

- People make different inferences in each of the eight emotional problems listed above.
- They disturb themselves by holding a set of irrational beliefs about these inferences. The nature of these irrational beliefs is that they are rigid and extreme.
- When people hold irrational beliefs, they do not only experience disturbed emotions, they also act (or feel like acting) in certain dysfunctional ways and think in highly distorted ways. These thinking and behavioural consequences of irrational beliefs give expression to these beliefs and tend to reinforce people's conviction in the irrational beliefs that spawn them.
- People can hold irrational beliefs at both the specific and general levels of abstraction. Their general irrational beliefs influence the inferences that they make in the first instance and then they bring their specific irrational beliefs to these inferences in the second to create their emotional problems and the

thinking and behaviours that accompany these problems. As you will see, the thinking and behaviours that stem from irrational beliefs vary according to the emotional problem under consideration.

The structure of each chapter is quite similar. While this may be repetitive, it will facilitate comparisons across the emotional problems and help you to see what is similar and what is different from problem to problem.

For ease of reading, I have not included academic or self-help references in the text. Rather, after each chapter, I have provided a key reference for you to consult according to your specific academic interests. I have also provided a key self-help reference for your clients.

Finally, with respect to gender and the singular/plural issue, I have used the female singular when discussing the relevant issues, unless the specific examples indicate otherwise. This was decided by a toss of the coin.

Windy Dryden
London and Eastbourne
April, 2008

Chapter 1

Understanding anxiety

In this chapter, I will make some general observations about anxiety before discussing more specific areas of this disabling emotion.

General points about anxiety

In this section, I will discuss:

- the role of threat in anxiety
- the role of a general anxiety-creating philosophy comprising four general irrational beliefs in general anxiety
- the role of specific irrational beliefs about specific threats in specific instances of anxiety.

In order to feel anxious a person needs to think that she is about to face a threat

In order to feel anxious a person needs to think that she is about to face some kind of threat. Without making a threat-related inference, the person won't feel psychologically anxious.

There are two different kinds of threats that a person may experience: threats to ego aspects of her personal domain and threats to non-ego aspects of her personal domain. As Aaron T. Beck (1976) noted in his book, *Cognitive Therapy and the Emotional Disorders*, the personal domain includes anything that a person holds dear. So when a person faces an ego threat, she is facing a threat to something that she holds dear, which has an impact on her self-esteem (e.g. she thinks that she might fail an examination, which if she did you would consider her to be a failure). When a person faces a non-ego threat, she is facing a threat to something that she holds dear, which does not have an impact on her self-esteem (e.g. she thinks that she might feel sick and she believes that she cannot bear experiencing such a feeling). It is important to note that a threat does not have to be real for a person to feel anxiety. The important point here is that the person herself considers the threat to be real.

A general anxiety-creating philosophy (GAP) underpins general anxiety

While locating a threat is a necessary condition for a person to feel anxious, it is not sufficient for the person to feel anxious. Some people, for example, feel concerned rather than anxious about the possibility of facing a threat. In order to experience anxiety about the real and imagined threats in her life, a person needs what I call a 'general anxiety-creating philosophy' (GAP).

There are four components to such a philosophy, and in my experience a person needs two of the four to ensure that she will become anxious. Let me review these components one at a time.

A rigid demand

When a person holds a rigid demand about threats, she asserts that these threats must not exist. For example, Sally is generally anxious about going for a health check and identifies a threat in that category (i.e. discovering that she is ill). Since Sally holds a rigid demand, she insists that she must not be ill. By demanding that something that may occur absolutely must not occur, Sally experiences the following consequences:

Emotional consequences

Sally experiences anxiety.

Thinking consequences

Sally's subsequent thinking is skewed and very distorted. She is so preoccupied with the possibility that she is ill that she excludes the possibility that she may be well and all she can think about concerns illness. In other words, Sally has tunnel vision that serves to sustain her anxiety.

Behavioural consequences

Sally's behaviour is characterised by avoidance. She avoids going for health checks. This will have the effect of reinforcing her idea that it would be absolutely horrible to be ill. If it wasn't horrible, she reasons, she wouldn't avoid going for health checks.

I will discuss the thinking and behavioural consequences of anxiety-related irrational beliefs more fully later in the chapter.

Rigid demands would make sense if they actually removed the possibility of facing a threat. Thus, if by demanding that she must not be ill, Sally removed the possibility of being ill, then making this demand would make sense. However, making demands has no such effect on reality. They don't magically remove the possibility of threats existing.

An awfulising belief

The second component of a general anxiety-creating philosophy (GAP) is known as an awfulising belief. When a person holds such a belief, she asserts that it would be horrible, awful, terrible or the end of the world for the threat to exist in the first place and for it to occur in the second place. Here, the person converts her sensible, non-extreme conclusions – e.g. in Sally's case that it would be bad or unfortunate to be ill – into illogical extreme conclusions – that it would be absolutely dreadful or the end of the world to be ill.

When Sally holds an awfulising belief and she thinks of going for health checks, for example, she tells herself that if she was ill, nothing could be worse than this and if it did happen, absolutely no good could possibly come from such an eventuality.

A low frustration tolerance belief

The third component of a general anxiety-creating philosophy (GAP) is known as a low frustration tolerance (LFT) belief. Here, the person asserts that she wouldn't be able to bear or tolerate it if the threat were to materialise. Thus, Sally's anxiety is underpinned by her telling herself that it would be intolerable for her to be ill. When she holds this belief, she pictures herself crumpled up in a heap on being told that she is ill and thinks that she will lose the capacity for happiness if she were ill.

A self-depreciation belief

As mentioned above, there are two basic forms of anxiety: ego anxiety, where a person makes herself anxious about a threat to her self-esteem, and non-ego anxiety, where she makes herself anxious about threats to things that do not involve self-esteem. In the latter type of anxiety, non-ego anxiety, a person generally holds a rigid demand and then either an awfulising belief or an LFT belief is most dominant in her thinking. Putting this diagrammatically we have:

Non-ego anxiety = Threat to non-ego aspect of personal domain × Rigid demand + Awfulising belief

or

Non-ego anxiety = Threat to non-ego aspect of personal domain × Rigid demand + LFT belief

In ego anxiety, a person generally holds a rigid demand and a self-depreciation belief as shown below:

Ego anxiety = Threat to ego aspect of personal domain × Rigid demand + Self-depreciation belief

When a person holds a self-depreciation belief, she makes a global negative rating, judgement or evaluation about her entire self (e.g. 'I am a failure'; 'I am less worthy'; 'I am unlovable').

For example, Norman is anxious about receiving disapproval (a general category of events that, if they happened, would result in him lowering his self-esteem). Thus, receiving disapproval is, for Norman, an ego threat. Now if we add Norman's rigid demand and self-depreciation to this threat, we have: 'I must not be disapproved of and if I am this proves that I am an unlikeable person.'

***When a person is anxious in specific situations,
she focuses on a specific threat and practises a
specific version of her general anxiety-creating
philosophy***

When a person holds a general anxiety-creating philosophy (GAP), she increases the chances of identifying threats in her environment. This tendency to locate threats to her personal domain is characteristic of a person who experiences general anxiety. If a person only identified such threats when they actually existed, she would still make herself anxious, but wouldn't do so very often. To make herself anxious regularly and frequently, a person tends to be very sensitive to threats to her personal domain. GAPs sensitise a person to the possibility of threat in the absence of objective evidence that such threats actually exist.

Let me explain how holding a GAP influences a person's ability to identify threats in her environment, before listing common GAPs that, once internalised, will lead to much anxiety in a person's life.

Norman (who we met above) holds the following GAP: 'I must be approved by new people that I meet and if I'm not it proves that I am unlikeable.' Since Norman believes this, he will become preoccupied with the possibility that new people will not like him and will think that he is unlikeable, unless he is certain that they will like him. This preoccupation will involve Norman tending to do the following:

- He will tend to overestimate the chances that a new group of people won't approve of him and underestimate the chances that they will approve of him [overestimating the *probability* of disapproval].
- He will tend to think that if they do disapprove of him, they will disapprove of him greatly, rather than just mildly or moderately [overestimating the *degree* of disapproval].
- He will tend to think that all or most of those present will disapprove of him rather than the more realistic situation where some might disapprove of him, others might approve of him and yet others might be neutral towards him – assuming that he doesn't have crass social habits that will objectively antagonise all or most people he has just met [overestimating the *extent* of disapproval].

In summary, when a person holds a GAP about approval, for example, she will overestimate the probability, degree and extent of the opposite happening (i.e. being disapproved) in her environment. GAPs lead a person to become oversensitive to threat.

So far I have discussed the role that general anxiety-creating philosophies play in making a person oversensitive to threat in her environment. Once the person has identified a specific threat in a specific environment she will then hold a specific version of her GAP to make herself anxious in that specific situation. Let's take Norman's example again. He holds a GAP that I discussed above, namely: 'I must be approved by new people that I meet and if I'm not it proves that I am unlikeable.' Now let's further assume that Norman goes to a party where there are people that he doesn't know and his host is about to introduce him to these people. Norman's GAP will immediately lead him to focus on the threat in this situation, e.g. 'These specific people will not like me.' This is known as an inference. An inference is a hunch about reality that can be correct or incorrect, but a GAP leads a person to think of it as a fact.

Having focused on this specific threat, Norman needs to hold a specific version of his GAP. In this case, it is: 'These people that I am about to meet must not disapprove of me and if they do it means that I am unlikeable.' Holding this specific belief and applying it to the threat-related inference will mean that Norman will be anxious in the specific situation under consideration.

Focusing on and going with the behavioural and thinking consequences of irrational beliefs will serve to maintain anxiety

In summary, holding a general anxiety-creating philosophy will lead a person to seek out threats in her environment and she will make herself anxious about these threats by specific versions of her GAP. Anxiety, then, is the emotional consequence of this threat–irrational belief interaction as shown below:

Specific threat × Specific irrational belief = Emotional consequence:

• Anxiety

However, there are two other consequences of this threat–irrational belief interaction that serve to maintain and exacerbate anxiety. These are known as behavioural consequences and thinking consequences.

Behavioural consequences of irrational beliefs

Let's start with the behavioural consequences of the threat × irrational belief interaction. Thus, when Norman thinks that new people he is about to meet will disapprove of him (threat) and he demands that this must not happen and he is unlikeable if it does (irrational belief), then he may act or tend to act in a number of ways:

- He may tend to avoid meeting these new people [*avoiding* the threat].
- If Norman has to meet these new people, he may leave at the first opportunity [physically *withdrawing* from the threat].
- If Norman cannot leave the situation he may remain silent so that he doesn't do anything to provoke disapproval [*passive neutralising* of the threat].
- He may go out of his way to get approval from the people concerned [*active neutralising* of the threat].
- If Norman cannot leave the situation he may find some way of behaviourally distracting himself from the threat such as picking his hands [*behavioural distraction* from the threat].
- He may try to deal with the threat by overcompensating for it (e.g. by actively provoking disapproval to try to convince himself that he doesn't care if he is approved or not) [*behaviourally overcompensating* for the threat].

If Norman acts in one or more of the above ways, once he is anxious, then he will maintain his anxiety. By acting in such ways, Norman is actually rehearsing and thus strengthening his specific and general irrational beliefs. Thus, when Norman avoids being introduced to a new group of people, he implicitly thinks something like: 'If I were to meet these people, they might disapprove of me. They must not disapprove of me and if they do it means that I am unlikeable. Thus, I'll avoid meeting them.' And when a person strengthens her irrational beliefs about threat, she increases the likelihood that she will make herself anxious in future.

The following sums up what I have said in this section:

Specific threat × Specific irrational belief = Behavioural consequences:

- Avoiding the threat
- Physically withdrawing from the threat
- Passive neutralising of the threat
- Active neutralising of the threat
- Behavioural distraction from the threat
- Behaviourally ovecompensating for the threat

Thinking consequences of irrational beliefs

There are also thinking consequences of the threat–irrational belief interaction. These consequences are of two types. The first type involves the person elaborating on the threat. For example, when Norman thinks that new people he is about to meet will disapprove of him (threat) and he demands that this must not happen and he is unlikeable if it does (irrational belief), then he will tend to think in a number of ways:

- He will tend to think that the consequences of the disapproval that he predicts that he will receive will be highly negative. Thus, he may think that once the strangers disapprove of him then they will tell others about their negative views of him, that their disapproval of him will last a long time and that it may affect his chances of meeting new friends in the future [*exaggerating the negative consequences* of the predicted threat].
  This thinking consequence serves to increase Norman's anxiety because it gives him even more negative threats to think about while holding other specific irrational beliefs.

Other types of thinking consequences involve Norman trying to deal with the threat in a number of (ineffective) ways:

- He may try to distract himself from the threat by attempting to think of something else [*cognitive distraction* from the threat].
- He may attempt to overcompensate for the threat in his thinking by either imagining himself being indifferent to the disapproval or by thinking of himself gaining great approval in another (imaginary) setting [*cognitively overcompensating* for the threat].

These two thinking consequences serve to maintain anxiety in ways that are similar to the behavioural consequences I discussed earlier in that they implicitly give the person an opportunity to rehearse and thus strengthen her irrational belief. Thus, if Norman tries to distract himself from the possibility that a new group of people will not approve of him, he is largely doing so because he believes implicitly that they must approve of him and he is unlikeable if they don't. If he wasn't holding irrational beliefs about this threat, he would be more likely to think about the threat objectively and deal with it constructively if it actually occurred.

To sum up:

Specific threat × Specific irrational belief = Thinking consequences:

- Exaggerating the negative consequences of the predicted threat
- Cognitive distraction from the threat
- Cognitively overcompensating for the threat

How a person adds anxious insult to anxious injury

A person may unwittingly increase and deepen her anxiety by holding a specific anxiety-creating belief about different aspects of her anxiety with a specific anxiety-creating belief. Let me give you an example of what I mean.

Remember that Norman's GAP is: 'I must be approved by new people that I meet and if I'm not it proves that I am unlikeable.' He attends a social gathering where he is likely to be introduced to people that he doesn't know. Under these conditions, his GAP will lead him to identify a specific threat in this situation, namely that strangers at the gathering are likely to disapprove of him. He then brings a specific version of his GAP to this specific threat until he has made himself anxious. Then, and this is the important point, he may focus on some aspect of his anxiety and think about this using another specific anxiety-creating, irrational belief. Here are some examples of how Norman may unwittingly increase his anxiety in this way:

- *He may focus on his general feelings of anxiety* and tell himself: 'I must not be anxious, I can't stand feeling anxious and I have to get rid of it immediately.' This will increase his feelings of anxiety.

- *He may focus on a symptom of his anxiety* (such as his heart pounding) and tell himself: 'I must stop my heart pounding and it would be terrible if I don't.' This will increase his heart pounding and also make it more likely that he will think that he will have a heart attack if his palpitations increase – which they will if he holds such a belief.
- *He may focus on a behavioural consequence of his anxiety* (e.g. his urge to avoid meeting new people) and tell himself: 'I must not feel like avoiding this situation and because I do I am a weak wimp.'
- *He may focus on a thinking consequence of his anxiety* (e.g. that new people will laugh at me if I say something silly) and tell himself: 'New people must not laugh at me and if they do it proves that I am an utter fool.'

As a person keeps increasing her feelings of anxiety, her negative thoughts will become more dire and her urge to act in unconstructive ways will become more pressing. When this happens and she holds a specific irrational belief about each spiral, she will eventually get herself into a state of panic, her thoughts spiralling out of control and becoming evermore chaotic.

Understanding specific forms of anxiety

In this section, I will discuss the following specific forms of anxiety:

- anxiety about losing self-control
- anxiety about uncertainty
- health anxiety
- social anxiety
- panic attacks.

Anxiety about losing self-control

One of the most common themes in people's anxiety concerns losing self-control. This is not surprising since one of the things many of us take pride in is our ability to remain in control of ourselves and in particular of our feelings, our thoughts and our behaviour. When a person makes herself anxious about losing self-control, she holds a rigid demand about self-control in the area of her preoccupation. For example:

- 'I must not feel anxious' (loss of self-control of feelings).
- 'I must not think weird thoughts' (loss of self-control of thoughts).
- 'I must not have images that I find hard to dismiss' (loss of self-control of images).
- 'I must not have the urge to act in that way' (loss of self-control over urges to act).
- 'I must behave in a certain way' (loss of self-control over behaviour).

The above tend to be general anxiety-creating irrational beliefs. In a specific situation, a person brings a relevant, specific demand to an episode where she has begun to lose a bit of self-control. For example, take the case of Lara, who has started to have an image of throwing herself off a bridge. She tells herself that she must not have such a mental picture and that she must get rid of the image immediately. As a consequence of these irrational beliefs, Lara's image becomes more vivid and increases in aversiveness. Then Lara begins to think that unless she gains control of her images right now, she will go mad. She will then tend to avoid situations with which she associates losing control. Thus, she may well avoid going over bridges or even looking at pictures of bridges.

She may also avoid the subject of mental breakdown and pictures of psychiatric hospitals in an attempt to regain emotional control, but as she does so, she unwittingly strengthens her dire need for self-control. After a while, Lara will quickly jump in her mind from the beginning of losing self-control (e.g. beginning to have the image of throwing herself off a bridge) to the end where she has gone crazy. With practice, Lara develops the following irrational belief with the following thinking consequence. 'I must be in control of my mental processes at all times or I will go mad' (with the unspoken idea that it is terrible to go mad).

In cases of anxiety over losing self-control, people tend to have the idea that one's thoughts, feelings and urges to act are a good guide to reality. In Lara's case, if she thinks that she is going to throw herself off a bridge, then she will. Since she thinks that having the image of throwing herself off a bridge means that she is going to do it, in order to make herself safe, she thinks that she mustn't have such an image. Paradoxically, when a person demands that she must not have a thought or an image, then she makes it more likely that she will have such a thought or image. With such a demand, every intensification of the image leads Lara to redouble her demands to get rid of the image and soon all she will be able to think of is throwing herself off a bridge.

Anxiety about uncertainty

Many people make themselves anxious about uncertainty. Let me explain how this works by discussing the case of Cleo.

1   Cleo focuses on something uncertain that constitutes a threat to her (e.g. 'My children are 15 minutes late home and I don't know what has happened to them').

2   Cleo rehearses the belief that she must be sure that the threat does not exist and that it is awful not to have such certainty (e.g. 'I must know that my children are safe and it is awful not to know this').

3   Cleo practises the idea that uncertainty means that bad things will inevitably occur (e.g. 'Because I don't know that my children are safe and I must know this, not knowing that they are safe means that something bad has happened to them or that they at risk').

4   Cleo rehearses her awfulising belief about this occurrence (e.g. 'It would be awful if my children were not safe').

5   Cleo seeks reassurance from others that the threat really does not exist or she keeps checking to determine that the threat does not exist (e.g. Cleo keeps going to the window to check if she can see her children and she rings round their friends' parents to discover if they know her children's whereabouts).

6   Cleo then casts doubt on such reassurance ('When the parents of Cleo's children's friends try to reassure her that her children are OK, she is immediately reassured, but then she casts doubt on this saying such things to herself as 'How do they know?'; 'They are only saying this to reassure me'; 'I'm sure that they would be out of their mind with worry if it was their children who were late').

7   Cleo keeps a mental scrapbook of stories about the bad things that happen to children who are late home and ignores the

millions of unreported incidents of children being late home who were safe.

Health anxiety

Health anxiety occurs when a person thinks that she has a serious illness in the absence of convincing evidence to support her contention. In my view, it is a specific form of anxiety about uncertainty. I will use the example of Esther to show health anxiety in action.

1   Esther has the general irrational belief that she must know at all times that she does not have a serious disease and that it is terrible if she doesn't have such certainty. This belief leads Esther to become adept at identifying symptoms that could be signs of serious illness.
2   Esther focuses on a particular symptom that could be evidence of a serious illness (e.g. skin blemishes, lumps and pains). Recently, Esther identified a pain in her chest and brought a specific version of the above-mentioned general irrational belief to this specific situation (i.e. 'I must know now that this chest pain is not a sign of a heart attack and I can't bear not knowing this').
3   Esther thought that uncertainty in this context was a sign of serious illness.
4   She sought professional advice and when it was given and she was reassured that there is nothing seriously wrong with her, she cast doubt on this reassurance when her symptom persisted. She could not see that the continuation of her symptom was due to the attention that she gave to it, influenced as it is by her irrational belief. Rather, she accepted the view that states that such symptoms are exclusively due to organic, non-psychological symptoms.
    People with health anxiety frequently cast doubt on the validity of the medical opinion that they have been given that there is nothing wrong with them. They do so by:

•   Doubting the thoroughness of the examination [e.g. 'In retrospect the doctor only gave me a cursory examination and he (in this case) didn't ask me many questions about my symptoms. I really think that he missed something'].

- Doubting the state of the medical examiner when she (in this case) conducted the examination [e.g. 'Come to think of it the doctor looked pale and distracted when she was examining me. I really think that she missed something'].
- Doubting the competence of the medical examiner [e.g. 'I've heard a number of people say that the doctor who examined me is incompetent. I really think that he missed something'].

5   Esther consulted other medical examiners and cast doubt on the opinions given each time.

6   Esther asked her family and friends for reassurance, which only had a short-lived effect because she was not reassurable.

7   Esther consulted books on medical symptoms and visited sites on the World Wide Web in the hope of finding out that her symptoms were benign. However, she inevitably found something to support the view that she was seriously ill and when she found such information, she accepted it as true, at least in her case.

8   Esther kept checking to determine the status of her symptoms, which increased her health anxiety. Checking focused her attention on the symptoms that she was worried about and meant that she became more aware of them. Her increased attention led to an intensification of her symptoms. Then, as she thought her symptoms were getting worse, she brought her awfulising belief to this situation, which led her to conclude that she must be seriously ill.

   There are symptoms such as skin blemishes and lumps that get worse if a person physically checks on them. If the person awfulises about this 'deterioration', the person tends to conclude once again that she is seriously ill.

9   Esther acted as though she was seriously ill. Thinking that the chest pains that she had been experiencing meant that she was suffering from a heart condition, she stopped taking exercise and avoided situations that might raise her heart rate.

Social anxiety

Many people are anxious about social situations. Let me explain how this works by discussing the case of Steve.

1   When Steve gets to a relevant social situation, he remembers his ideal social behaviour and focuses on the fact that he will fall far short of such behaviour. Then he demands that he must act in accord with his ideal and that he is a worthless person if he doesn't.
2   He then thinks that others present will judge him negatively, but he doesn't look at them so that he can't disconfirm this inference.
3   While thinking that others are judging him negatively, Steve demands that they must not do this and if they do that this proves that he is worthless.
4   If Steve does go to social situations, he tends to keep himself to himself and does not initiate social contact with others. Consequently, he comes across as uninterested in others who do not attempt to talk to him. Steve focuses on this latter point, does not realise his role in keeping others away and thinks he is worthless because others do not talk to him.
5   If Steve avoids similar social situations in future, he keeps reminding himself that if he did go out socially he must come across well and he must be liked, otherwise he will be worthless.
6   Largely as a result of his social anxiety, Steve has developed poor social skills. In particular, he does not engage people in appropriate eye contact. He either stares at people for a long period of time or does not engage in eye contact with them at all.

Panic attacks

Panic attacks are a particularly painful form of anxiety. There are three core elements of a panic attack:

• The belief that you must not lose control and it is terrible if you do.
• The notion that when your symptoms increase this is evidence that you are facing an imminent internal catastrophe (e.g. a heart attack, a stroke, going mad, fainting, to name but a few).
• The idea that it is terrible to have a panic attack and that you must avoid doing so at all costs.

Let's take these points one at a time.
   The first foundation of a panic attack is an anxiety about anxiety philosophy. Henry is waiting to give a public presentation and

notices that he feels somewhat anxious and sweaty. When he tells himself that it is horrific to feel anxious and that he must gain control of it immediately, he then increases his anxiety. If every time Henry's anxiety increases he awfulises about it, then he will begin to feel that he is really losing control. When he get to this stage, then it will be very easy for him to demand that he must gain control immediately and that it will be terrible if he doesn't.

The second foundation of a panic attack involves the inference that an immediate, catastrophic internal event is likely to happen if the person doesn't gain immediate control. Common catastrophic inferences include having a heart attack, having a stroke or going mad in some way. Then the person tends to act in order to avoid such an event happening. For example, when Henry thought that he was going to have a stroke, at the point when he felt as if he was losing control, he sat down to stop himself (i.e. in his mind) from having one. In doing so, Henry calmed down because he thought that his action warded off having a stroke. He did this whenever he felt he was going to have a stroke and, in doing so, Henry never actually tested out the validity of his inference.

The third foundation of a panic attack is for the person to become anxious about having a panic attack. This is likely to happen under the following conditions:

- When the person rehearses the irrational belief that she must not experience a panic attack and it would be awful to do so.
- When the person thinks that wherever she goes she might have a panic attack and when she practises the above belief while thinking this.
- When the person avoids going to places where she thinks that she might have a panic attack.
- When the person takes steps to avoid having a panic attack if she cannot avoid going to such places (e.g. by using medication, drink and drugs).

A view of the world founded on anxiety-creating irrational beliefs renders a person particularly vulnerable to developing and maintaining anxiety

People develop views of the world as it relates to them that render them vulnerable to particular unhealthy negative emotions. This is certainly the case with anxiety. The world views that render a person vulnerable to anxiety do so primarily because they make it very easy for the person to make anxiety-related inferences. Then the person makes herself anxious about these inferences with the appropriate irrational beliefs. Here is an illustrative list of world views and the inferences that they spawn.

World view: The world is a dangerous place.
Inference: If a situation can be threatening, then it is threatening.

World view: Uncertainty is dangerous.
Inference: Not knowing that a threat does not exist means that it does.

World view: Not being in control is dangerous.
Inference: If I am not in control, then I will soon lose control completely.

World view: People can't be trusted.
Inference: People are unpredictable and will threaten me without warning.

Further reading

Academic

Barlow, D. (2002). *Anxiety and its disorders: The nature and treatment of anxiety and panic.* Second edition. New York: Guilford.

Self-help

Dryden, W. (2000). *Overcoming anxiety.* London: Sheldon.

Having discussed the REBT perspective on anxiety, in the next chapter I will discuss what it has to say about depression.

Chapter 2

Understanding depression

It is useful to distinguish between two types of depression: sociotropic depression and autonomous depression. In sociotropic depression a person is depressed about issues such as loss of affiliation, loss of love, loss of being connected to people and loss of relationships, whereas in autonomous depression, a person is depressed about losses of freedom, autonomy, competence and status. I will first discuss sociotropic depression before turning my attention to autonomous depression.

Sociotropic depression

In discussing sociotropic depression, I will consider:

- The role of general irrational beliefs.
- The impact of these beliefs on thinking about loss.
- Specific loss and specific irrational beliefs.
- The effect of irrational beliefs on behaviour and subsequent thinking.
- Metaphors and images in sociotropic depression.

The role of general irrational beliefs in sociotropic depression

When a person makes herself sociotropically depressed, she tends to hold a number of general irrational beliefs.

First, she tends to hold a *rigid demand* about the place of being liked, loved, connected to people in her life and the role that relationships play for her. For example:

- 'I must be liked.'
- 'I must be loved.'
- 'I must be connected to people that I care for.'
- 'I must have a special relationship in my life.'

Second, in some forms of sociotropic depression, a person tends to hold a *self-depreciation* belief about these issues. I call this type of depression self-worth sociotropic depression because in effect the person is basing her self-esteem on the presence of being liked, loved etc. For example:

- '[I must be liked] . . . and if I'm not, then I'm unlikeable.'
- '[I must be loved] . . . and if I'm not, then I'm unlovable.'
- '[I must be connected to people that I care about] . . . and if I'm not, then I am not worth caring about.'
- '[I must have a special relationship in my life] . . . and if I don't, then I'm a nobody.'

Third, in other forms of sociotropic depression (which I call non self-worth sociotropic depression), the person is not depreciating herself. Rather, she is disturbing herself about the resultant conditions that exist following her loss. For example:

- '[I must be liked] . . . and if I'm not, I couldn't bear it.'
- '[I must be loved] . . . and if I'm not, it's awful.'
- '[I must be connected to people that I care about] . . . and if I'm not, then I would disintegrate since I am too weak to look after myself.'
- '[I must have a special relationship in my life] . . . and if I don't, my life is nothing.'

As can be seen, some of these beliefs are dependency beliefs, which are a major feature of non self-worth sociotropic depression.

Focusing on sociotropic loss

If a person holds general irrational beliefs about loss with respect to being liked, loved etc., and these are triggered in some way, they will tend to lead the person to focus on such loss in her mind. Such a loss can be a past loss where the person recalls from memory a specific time when she thought she was rejected, disliked or disconnected. Or alternatively, she can review her present relationships and focus on one which isn't going too well, bring a relevant irrational belief to this relationship until she concludes that the other person doesn't like her, doesn't love her or wants to reject her.

Bringing a specific irrational belief to a specific sociotropic loss

Once a person has focused on a loss and made herself depressed about it, the person has brought a specific version of her general irrational belief to this loss. For example, Beryl identified a recent situation where she thought Rosemary, a friend, acted coolly towards her. Using her general irrational belief – 'My friends must always show interest in me and if they don't, it proves that I am an unlikeable person', she translated this 'cool action' into the inference that Rosemary rejected her. Focusing on this specific loss, Beryl brought to it a specific version of her general belief, namely: 'Rosemary must not reject me and because she did, I am an unlikeable person.'

The same process occurs when a person experiences an actual sociotropic loss. She focuses on this loss while holding a specific irrational belief and in this way makes herself sociotropically depressed.

The effects of irrational beliefs on behaviour

When a person feels sociotropically depressed, this impacts on her behaviour. In other words, a person will tend to act in ways that are consistent with her depressed mood. In Beryl's example:

- She avoided Rosemary and other friends.
- She stayed away from enjoyable activities.
- She played depressing music, read depressing novels or poetry (particularly those that deal with rejection).
- She talked to people who were also depressed.

The effects of irrational beliefs on subsequent thinking

One important effect of depression-related irrational beliefs is that it has a decided negative effect on a person's subsequent thinking. Let me outline and exemplify some of the thinking errors that *stem from* or *follow from* Beryl's specific irrational belief: 'Rosemary must not reject me and because she did, I am an unlikeable person.' These thinking errors had a deepening effect on Beryl's depression.

In outlining these thinking errors, I will show how they stem from the irrational beliefs in underlined text.

- *Black and white thinking* [Taking an event and putting it into one of two black and white categories]: 'You either like me or you dislike me. There is no other way of looking at it. Since Rosemary has rejected me on this occasion, as she absolutely should not have done, this means that she doesn't like me.'

- *Overgeneralisation* [Taking an event and generalising it to all other similar situations and relevant categories]: 'Since Rosemary rejected me, as she absolutely should not have done, all my friends will reject me.'

- *Always–never thinking* [Taking an event and thinking that it will be like this forever or it will never change]: 'Since Rosemary rejected me, as she absolutely should not have done, I'll never be friends with Rosemary again. I'll always be rejected by my friends.'

- *Exaggeration* [Using an event as a springboard to make extreme and exaggerated statements about it and matters relating to it]: 'Since Rosemary rejected me, as she absolutely should not have done, nobody truly likes me.'

- *Negative prediction* [Taking an event and making negative predictions about it and matters relating to it]: 'Since Rosemary rejected me, as she absolutely should not have done, whoever I make friends with in the future will reject me.'

- *Ignoring the positive*: [Taking an event and making that event colour everything in your life so that you ignore the positive]: 'The fact that I got a good review at work doesn't matter. The only thing that matters is that Rosemary has rejected me, as she absolutely should not have done.'

- *Helplessness* [Editing out your personal resourcefulness to change matters on a broad scale]: 'Since Rosemary rejected me, as she absolutely should not have done, I can't do anything to get people to like me. They are capable of liking me, but I don't have the resources of getting them to like me.'

- *Hopelessness* [Seeing no hope for the future]: 'Since Rosemary rejected me, as she absolutely should not have done, I'll be emotionally alone in the future. I have the resources to change matters, but they just can't be changed.'

A particularly potent combination of thinking errors in the deepening of depression is helplessness and hopelessness. In this context, a person shows herself that she doesn't have the resources to get people to like her (helplessness) and even if she did it wouldn't change anything (hopelessness).

Bringing irrational beliefs to subsequent thinking

Once a person has created a particular thinking error by holding a specific irrational depression-creating belief about a loss, she may then deepen her depression by focusing on the content of her thinking error from the perspective of another specific irrational belief. For example, Beryl created the following thinking error and is now focusing on it: 'Whoever I make friends with in the future will reject me.' She brings the following irrational belief to this error, thus: 'People must not keep rejecting me and if they do it proves that I am completely worthless.'

What will in all probability happen is that the person's subsequent thinking will be even more negative and distorted (e.g. 'I will always be alone. I will never be connected to another human being again. Life will always be bleak and hopeless'). This will lead to hopelessness about the future.

Metaphors and images in sociotropic depression

When a person is in a sociotropic depression, she will tend to create and dwell on images or metaphors that illustrate how she feels. Here are some examples of such images and metaphors that depict the hopelessness of sociotropic depression:

- 'I am in solitary isolation with no way out.'
- 'I see others enjoying themselves and I have no way of reaching them.'
- 'I am trapped in a loveless existence.'

If the person rehearses such metaphors and images then she will maintain and even deepen her sense of hopelessness.

Autonomous depression

As I pointed out earlier in this chapter, there are two types of depression: sociotropic depression and autonomous depression. If you recall, in sociotropic depression, the person is depressed about issues such as loss of affiliation, loss of love, loss of being connected to people and loss of relationships, whereas in autonomous depression the person is depressed about losses of freedom, autonomy, competence and status. In this section, I will discuss autonomous depression.

The role of general irrational beliefs in autonomous depression

When a person makes herself autonomously depressed, she tends to hold a number of general irrational beliefs.

First, she tends to hold a *rigid demand* about the place of achieving key goals and standards in her life such as achievement, being competent, self-reliant, autonomous and having high status. For example:

- 'I must achieve what I want in life.'
- 'I must be competent.'
- 'I must be able to determine my life path free from external restrictions.'
- 'I must be self-reliant.'
- 'I must achieve the status in life that I have set for myself.'

Second, in some forms of autonomous depression, the person tends to hold a *self-depreciation* belief about these issues. I call this type of depression self-worth autonomous depression because in effect the person is basing her self-esteem on the presence of conditions such as achievement, competence, self-reliance, autonomy and status.

- '[I must achieve what I want in life] . . . and if I don't, then I am a failure.'
- '[I must be competent] . . . and if I'm not, then I am an idiot.'
- '[I must be able to determine my life path free from external restrictions] . . . and if I can't, then I am a useless person.'
- '[I must be self-reliant] . . . and if I'm not, then I am a weak person.'
- '[I must achieve the status in life that I set for myself] . . . and if I don't, then I am worthless.'

Third, in other forms of autonomous depression (which I call non self-worth autonomous depression), the person is not depreciating herself. Rather, she is disturbing herself about the resultant conditions that exist following her loss.

- '[I must achieve what I want in life] . . . and if I don't, I couldn't bear it.'
- '[I must be competent] . . . and if I'm not, it's awful.'
- '[I must be able to determine my life path free from external restrictions] . . . and if I am not able to, it's intolerable.'
- '[I must be self-reliant] . . . and it's the end of the world if I'm not.'
- '[I must achieve the status in life that I have set for myself] . . . and if I don't, I couldn't stand it.'

Focusing on autonomous loss

If a person holds general irrational beliefs about loss with respect to failing, being constrained, losing status etc., and these are triggered in some way, they will tend to lead the person to focus on such loss in her mind. Thus, as in sociotropic depression, her specific autonomous loss can be a past loss where she recalls from memory a specific time when she was or thought she was incompetent or controlled by others. Or alternatively she can review her present life and focus on an autonomous area which isn't going too well, evaluate this situation with a relevant irrational belief as detailed above until she concludes that she has experienced a significant loss.

Bringing a specific irrational belief to a specific autonomous loss

Once a person has focused on an autonomous loss and has made herself depressed about it, the person has brought a specific version of her general irrational belief to this loss. Thus, Edwina identified a recent situation where she had been taken off a project at work by her boss. Using her general irrational belief – 'I must be able to determine my fate and it's terrible if I can't' – she translated being taken off the project into the inference that her fate was being determined by her boss. Focusing on this specific loss, Edwina brought to it a specific version of her general belief, namely: 'My boss must not determine my fate and it's terrible if he does.'

The effects of irrational beliefs on behaviour

When a person feels autonomously depressed, this impacts on her behaviour. In other words, a person will tend to act in ways that are consistent with her depressed mood. In Edwina's example:

- She avoided seeing her boss to present a case for remaining on the project.
- She gave up working on other projects to which she had been assigned.
- She played depressing music, read depressing novels or poetry (especially those where the protagonists are constrained).
- She talked to people who were also depressed about how their bosses determine what they do at work.

The effects of irrational beliefs on subsequent thinking

As I said earlier, depression-related irrational beliefs influence a person's subsequent thinking in that it becomes highly distorted in negative ways. These thinking errors will serve to deepen depression. Let me show the types of thinking that *stem from* Edwina's specific depression-related autonomy irrational belief: 'My boss must not determine my fate and it's terrible if he does.' These thinking errors had a deepening effect on Edwina's depression. In outlining these thinking errors, I will show how they stem from the irrational beliefs in underlined text.

- *Black and white thinking* [Taking an event and putting it into one of two black and white categories]: 'Since my boss has taken me off the project, which he absolutely should not have done, he is completely in control of my destiny since I am either in control of my fate or I am controlled by another person.'
- *Overgeneralisation* [Taking an event and generalising it to all other similar situations and relevant categories]: 'Since my boss is in control of my destiny in this situation, which he absolutely should not be, he is in control of my destiny in all work-related situations.'
- *Always–never thinking* [Taking an event and thinking that it will be like this forever or it will never change]: 'Since my boss

has taken me off the project, <u>which he absolutely should not have done</u>, I'll never be in charge of my fate again. I'll always be under the control of this boss and other bosses.'

- *Exaggeration* [Using an event as a springboard to make extreme and exaggerated statements about it and matters relating to it]: 'Since my boss has taken me off the project, <u>which he absolutely should not have done</u>, my life is ruined if I don't have complete control of my fate, <u>which I must have</u>.'

- *Negative prediction* [Taking an event and making negative predictions about it and matters relating to it]: 'Since my boss has taken me off the project, <u>which he absolutely should not have done</u>, wherever I work, my destiny will not be my own.'

- *Ignoring the positive* [Taking an event and making that event colour everything in your life so that you ignore the positive]: 'The fact that there are other areas of work where I do have control does not matter, the only thing that matters is that my boss has taken me off the project, <u>which he absolutely should not have done</u>.'

- *Helplessness* [Editing out your personal resourcefulness to change matters on a broad scale]: 'Since my boss has taken me off the project, <u>which he absolutely should not have done</u>, I can't do anything to change this. Something could be done about it, but I don't have the resources to do it.'

- *Hopelessness* [Seeing no hope for the future]: 'Since my boss has taken me off the project, <u>which he absolutely should not have done</u>, no matter what happens, others will be in charge of my fate. I have the resources to change matters, but they can't be changed.'

As before, the last two thinking errors represent a particularly potent combination in the deepening of depression.

Bringing irrational beliefs to subsequent thinking

Once a person has created a particular thinking error by holding a specific irrational depression-creating belief about an autonomous loss, she may then deepen her depression by focusing on the content of her thinking error from the perspective of another specific irrational belief. For example, Edwina created the following thinking error and is now focusing on it: 'Wherever I work my destiny will not be my own.' She brings the following irrational belief to this error: 'Wherever I work my destiny must be my own and if it's not it is completely intolerable.'

What will in all probability happen is that the person's subsequent thinking will be even more negative and distorted (e.g. 'I won't be able to control my destiny in life. Life will always be bleak and hopeless'). This will lead to hopelessness about the future.

Metaphors and images in autonomous depression

When a person is in an autonomously depressed frame of mind, she will tend to create and dwell on images or metaphors that illustrate how she feels. Here are some examples of such images and metaphors that depict the hopelessness of autonomous depression:

- 'My life is full of failure and defeat.'
- 'I see others succeeding and reaching their goals, but I have no chance of doing likewise.'
- 'I am a puppet and other people are pulling my strings.'
- 'I see myself in a nightmare where I can't look after myself, so others have to look after me.'

If the person rehearses such metaphors and images then she will maintain and even deepen her sense of hopelessness.

How depression deepens: the interaction of sociotropic and autonomous depression

I have now explained sociotropic and autonomous depression from an REBT perspective. This knowledge can be used to understand the deepening of depression when these two different types interact.

How a person can make himself autonomously depressed after he has made himself sociotropically depressed

Starting with sociotropic depression, let me show how a person can use this type of depression to make himself (in this case) autonomously depressed as well. Let's take the case of Ralph. He thought that his boss was annoyed with him and he made himself sociotropically depressed about this because he brought the following specific irrational belief to this presumed annoyance: 'My boss must not be annoyed with me and if she is, then this proves that I am unlikeable.' As I showed earlier in this chapter, holding a sociotropic depression-related irrational belief leads a person to think in ways that are negative and distorted in nature. The *content* of the thinking errors listed in that section that stem from sociotropic depression-related irrational beliefs is sociotropic in nature. Thus, in the example that I am using here when Ralph's boss, in his mind, demonstrated annoyance at him and he believed that she must not be annoyed at him and he is unlikeable if she does, he is likely to have such thoughts as: 'If my boss is annoyed at me, others will be too', which are sociotropic in content.

For a person to make himself depressed autonomously after he has made himself depressed sociotropically, he first needs to make the thinking that stems from his sociotropic depression-related irrational belief autonomous in nature. Thus, if the person believes that his boss must not be annoyed with him and he is unlikeable if she is, then when he focuses on his boss being annoyed at him, an example of an autonomous-related thinking consequence of this belief is: 'I will not advance in my career if my boss is annoyed with me.'

If Ralph then focuses on this distorted autonomous thought, treats it as if it were true and brings an autonomously related irrational belief to it, such as 'I must advance in my career and it's terrible if I don't', doing so will have the following effects:

- Ralph will feel autonomously depressed (don't forget that he already feels sociotropically depressed).
- Subsequently, he will tend to think such distorted autonomous-related thoughts as: 'There's no point in me working hard since I will never advance in my career.'
- He will tend to give up working hard at work, thereby increasing the chances of not getting promoted.

How a person can make himself autonomously depressed after he has made himself sociotropically depressed

Now let me show how a person can make himself sociotropically depressed after he has made himself autonomously depressed. Let's take the case of Derek, who thinks he is struggling at work. He makes himself autonomously depressed about this because he brings the following belief to this 'struggle': 'I must always do well at work and if I don't, then I am a failure.' Again, holding an autonomous depression-related irrational belief will lead a person to think subsequently in ways that are negative and distorted in nature and that the content of such thinking will be largely autonomous. Derek's subsequent autonomous-based thinking was 'Because I am struggling at work, I'll lose my job.'

For a person to make himself depressed sociotropically after he has made himself depressed autonomously, he first needs to make the thinking that stems from his autonomous depression-related irrational belief sociotropic in nature. Thus, if the person believes that he must always do well at work and he is a failure if he doesn't, then when he focuses on struggling at work, an example of a sociotropic-related thinking consequence of this belief is: 'My work colleagues will shun me once they see that I am struggling.'

If Derek then focuses on this distorted sociotropic thought, treats it as if it were true and brings a sociotropically related irrational belief to it, such as: 'I must have good relations with my work colleagues and if I don't, then I am unlikeable', doing so will have the following effects:

- Derek will feel sociotropically depressed (don't forget that he already feels autonomously depressed).
- Subsequently, he will tend to think such distorted sociotropic-related thoughts as: 'If my work colleagues don't want to know me, nobody will want to know me.'
- He will tend to withdraw socially, thereby increasing the chances of losing contact with people and of thinking that nobody wants to know him.

Self- and other-pity

Self- and other-pity are key are key components in some forms of depression. Let me consider these one at a time.

Self-pity

When a person feels sorry for herself (rather than for the bad position that she is in), she tends to take the following steps:

1   She tends to focus on an aspect of her life where she considers that she has been treated badly or where she has failed to

achieve something that she has worked very hard for. In particular, this aspect tends to be one where the person clearly thinks that (a) she did not deserve the bad treatment and (b) she deserved to achieve what she was striving for. In addition, the person is more likely to experience self-pity in these selected aspects where, in the first case, others who in her view deserved bad treatment actually received good treatment and where, in the second case, others who in her view had not worked as hard as her achieved what she wanted to achieve.

2   She tends to bring the following irrational belief to these situations (which may or may not be accurate):

- 'I must not be treated badly when I don't deserve to be (and when others who do deserve to be treated badly aren't) and when this occurs (a) it's terrible and (b) the world is a rotten place for allowing this to happen to a poor undeserving person like me.'
- 'When I work hard for something I must get what I think I deserve (particularly when others, who don't deserve to, get what I should have got) and when I don't (a) it's terrible and (b) the world is a rotten place for allowing this to happen to a poor undeserving person like me.'

3   She tends to use these irrational beliefs to influence her subsequent thinking. As I have already shown in this book, once a person brings an irrational belief to a threat to or a loss from her personal domain, then this belief influences her subsequent thinking in highly distorted negative ways.

   Thus, when a person thinks that she has undeservedly been treated badly and she holds an irrational belief about this as shown in (a) above, then she will tend to:

- Think about all the other occasions where she has been treated badly when she hasn't merited such treatment.
- Focus on all the unfairnesses that she has suffered and edit out all the unfairnesses that have been in her favour (which she probably thinks of as fairnesses).

When the person has worked hard for something and hasn't been awarded it and others less deserving of the award have received it, and she holds an irrational belief about this as detailed in (b) above, then she will tend to:

- Think about all the other occasions when all her hard work failed to be rewarded and edit out all the occasions when she has been rewarded for not working particularly hard.
- Think about all the occasions when others have been rewarded for not working particularly hard and edit out occasions when their hard labours or efforts have also not been rewarded.

She can then bring further irrational beliefs to these distorted thoughts to deepen her 'poor me' depression even further.

4   She tends to seek out people who are likely to share her 'unhealthy' views about unfairness and tell them about her hard luck story. In all probability they will respond with statements containing or implying irrational beliefs (e.g. 'Oh my God, poor you. How terrible for you'). The person will probably react to such statements positively because they validate her way of looking at things and will tend to use such 'other-pity' statements also to strengthen her conviction in self-pity related irrational beliefs.

Other-pity

When a person feels sorry for others (rather than for their plight), she tends to take the following steps:

1   She focuses on an aspect of life where she considers that other people are being treated very badly through no fault of their own. Other-pity is particularly experienced where these other people are clearly helpless victims (e.g. cruelty or abusive behaviour towards a child).

2   She tends to bring the following irrational belief to these situations (which may or may not be accurate):

- 'The world must not allow such bad treatment to happen and because it does the world is a rotten place. It is the end of the world for such treatment to be meted out to the poor person (or people)'.

3   She tends to use this irrational belief to influence her subsequent thinking. Thus, when she thinks that others have been treated badly through no fault of their own and she holds an

irrational belief about this (as shown above), then she will tend to:

- Focus on all the unfairnesses and bad treatment that innocent 'victims' have had to endure and edit out all the fairnesses that others have benefited from. In short, she focuses on man's inhumanity to man and edits out man's humanity to man. If the person keeps a scrapbook of such inhumane treatment and records news stories and documentaries of this ilk, she will reinforce this biased view of the world.
- Think that the world is getting worse in this respect and that there is no hope for humankind.

She will then tend to bring further irrational beliefs to these distorted thoughts to deepen her 'other-pity' depression even further.

4   She will tend, once again, to seek out people who are likely to share her 'unhealthy' views about the 'absolute horror' and 'intolerability' of man's inhumanity to man or swap 'horror' stories with them. Their unhealthy responses will tend to confirm the person's belief that the world is a horrible place and reinforce her biased view of the world.

5   She will tend to be passive and complain externally and internally about how horrible the world is rather than doing anything practical that might help these innocent 'victims'.

Depression about depression

As humans, we have the ability not only to disturb ourselves, but to disturb ourselves about our disturbances. There are many ways that a person can depress herself about her depression and in this part of this chapter I will cover two main ways.

How a person can depress herself about the physical aspects of depression

Depression can be physically painful. A person may, for example, have difficulty sleeping, she may lose her appetite and she may even have physical aches and pains.

When a person further depresses herself about the physical aspects of her depression, she tends to:

- Focus on the physical aspects of her depression.
- Bring the following irrational belief to these aspects: 'I must not feel so bad and I can't bear doing so.'
- Engage in the behavioural and thinking consequences of this belief:

Behavioural consequence: Remain inert and don't do anything enjoyable. This will have the effect of having the person focus even more on the increased physical pain of her deepening depression.

Thinking consequence: 'I'll never get over this pain. It is just unremitting.'

Self-depreciation about depression

- A person can depreciate herself about depressing herself in the first place in a number of ways. I will group these ways together.
- The person focuses on what being depressed means for her, e.g. a weakness, a failing, an evidence of having an unlovable trait.
- She then brings to this inference one of the following irrational beliefs and engages in the illustrative behavioural and thinking consequences of this belief.

'I must not be weak (by being depressed) and the fact that I have such a weakness means that I am a weak person.'

Behavioural consequence: Hides away from people.

Thinking consequence: Thinks of past instances when she has been weak. Thinks that she will always be weak.

'Being depressed means that I am failing and I must not fail in this respect and the fact that I have failed proves that I am a failure.'

Behavioural consequence: Doesn't try anything in case she fails.

Thinking consequence: Focuses on past failures. Thinks that she will always fail.

'Being depressed demonstrates that I have an unlovable trait that I must not have. Because I have, it proves that I am an unlovable person'

Behavioural consequence: Stays away from loved ones when depressed; tries to put on a brave face when with loved ones.

Thinking consequence: Thinks that she is bound to be rejected by anyone that she cares for if they see that she is depressed.

People develop and rehearse a view of the world founded on depression-based irrational beliefs

I mentioned in the previous chapter that people develop world views that render them vulnerable to particular unhealthy negative emotions. This is certainly the case with depression. The world views that render a person vulnerable to depression do so primarily because they make it very easy for her to make unhealthy depression-related inferences. Then, as I have shown you earlier in the chapter, the person makes herself depressed about these inferences with the appropriate irrational beliefs. Here is an illustrative list of world views that a person may develop and rehearse and the inferences that they spawn.

World view: Life is meaningless.
Inference: No matter what I do, ultimately it is meaningless.

World view: People will ultimately reject me.
Inference: If people get to know the real me, they will reject me.

World view: The world is made up of strong and weak people.
Inference: If I am not strong and independent, I am weak and dependent.

Preparing the ground for depression

Depression is very much experienced physically and therefore in order for a person to feel depressed, she will unwittingly tend to prepare the ground so that her depressed feelings take root. If a person does the following, she will make herself particularly vulnerable to depression:

- She doesn't wash and walks around all day wearing only her pyjamas/nightgown.
- She reads only the bad news in daily newspapers.
- She plays as many songs written by Leonard Cohen as she can find.

- She withdraws from any events that she is likely to enjoy. She only attends events where there is a very good chance of feeling depressed, either during the event or after it is finished. Even if she does enjoy the event, she points out to herself that she used to enjoy such events a lot more.
- She does things that she is likely to fail at and avoids doings things that she is likely to be successful at. If she does succeed at anything, she points out to herself either that (a) she used to do such things much better than she does now and/or (b) if she can do it, then anybody can do it.

Further reading

Academic

Gotlib, I.H. & Hammen, C. (Eds.). (2002). *Handbook of depression.* New York: Guilford.

Self-help

Dryden, W. & Opie, S. (2003). *Overcoming depression.* London: Sheldon.

Having discussed the REBT perspective on depression, in the next chapter I will discuss what it has to say about shame.

Chapter 3

Understanding shame

Shame and guilt are often linked together in people's minds and are often seen as similar emotions. While there are certain similarities to these two emotions, they also have important differences and as such they warrant a chapter each. Consequently, I will show you how a person makes herself feel ashamed in this chapter and feel guilty in the next.

How a person makes herself feel ashamed: general steps

In order for a person to feel ashamed and maintain these feelings, she tends to do the following:

1   She makes a shame-related inference.
2   She brings a shame-based irrational belief to that inference.
3   She thinks in ways that are consistent with the above irrational beliefs.
4   She acts in ways that are consistent with these irrational beliefs.
5   She rehearses a general version of her specific shame-based irrational beliefs so that she routinely makes shame-based inferences about what is generally going on in her life.
6   She develops and rehearses a shame-based world view.

So let me deal with these issues one at a time.

Shame-related inferences

In order to feel ashamed, a person needs to make one or more inferences about what is going on in her life. It is important to note that these inferences do not have to reflect accurately what is happening or what has happened. The important point is that she has to believe that they are true. Here is a list of common shame-related inferences:

'I've fallen short of my ideal'

When a person feels ashamed she focuses on some aspect of her life where she considers that she has fallen short (often very short) of her ideal, particularly in relation to some social code. Shame is often experienced when others are physically present, but if they are not, then she can still feel ashamed if she imagines that they are present or that they have discovered what she did (or did not do).

People who feel ashamed do so because they infer that they have fallen short in their behaviour, in what they think or imagine, in what they feel, or in some aspect of their physical self. Let me unpack and exemplify this statement.

The person focuses on her behaviour. This could concern what she did or what she failed to do. Here are some examples:

- She identifies something that she did that constitutes a weakness in her eyes (e.g. crying in public, acting foolishly in public).
- She identifies an incident where she broke a social code (e.g. she spoke about a taboo topic in front of a group of people).
- She identifies an incident where she failed to live up to her social code (e.g. she considers it to be important to treat people politely, but failed to treat a waiter with politeness).

The person focuses on her thoughts and images. Here are some examples of thoughts and images that people feel ashamed about:

- She thinks of harming her child.
- She pictures herself having sex with a member of her own gender when she is not gay.
- She thinks 'blasphemous' thoughts.

The person focuses on her emotions and how she expresses them. Some examples are:

- She feels unhealthily angry towards significant others.
- She shows her anger in a 'nasty' way.

- She feels maliciously envious towards a friend for being pregnant.
- She demonstrates her unhealthy jealousy in public.

The person focuses on her body. Here, the person might feel ashamed of some aspect of her body that she considers to be particularly unattractive. For example:

- A nose that she considers to be too big.
- Buttocks and/or thighs that she considers to be too fat.
- Breasts that she considers too large or too small.

'I've let down my reference group'

A reference group is a group with whom a person closely identifies. A person probably has a number of reference groups in her life, for example her family, friendship groups, her religious group and her cultural group. Each of these groups have 'let down' rules – behavioural rules that if the person breaks, the group would consider that she has let them down. As with other inferences, the inference that she has let down a reference group may or may not be accurate.

When a person feels ashamed about letting down a reference group, then:

- She breaks a 'let down' rule of a valued reference group.
- She thinks that the group 'feels' let down by her.

Here are some examples of how a person can let down her reference group:

- Marry out of her religion.
- Get caught stealing.
- Display emotion in public.

'I've been let down by a member of my reference group'

A person may also feel ashamed when a member of her reference group has broken one of the group's 'let down' rules and then thinks that the person has let her and the group down. Typical examples are the same as those listed above, namely where the other has:

- Married out of the person's religion.
- Got caught stealing.
- Displayed emotion in public.

'Others are judging me negatively'

It is difficult for a person to feel ashamed without making the inference that another person, but more frequently a group of people, judge her negatively. Again, whether or not these people are actually making such negative judgements is not as important as whether the person thinks they are. The person's feelings of shame are more likely to be acute if the group judging her negatively is physically present, but such feelings can also be present if she thinks about the group making such negative judgements.

What type of judgements does a person think others make of her when she feels ashamed? Here is a sample:

- Others communicate their displeasure at the person directly.
- Others communicate their disgust at the person directly.
- Others turn away from the person in disgust.
- Others demonstrate that they look down on the person.
- Others ignore the person.

The person holds and rehearses irrational beliefs about her shame-related inference

If there is a main point that I want to stress in this book it is this: at the core of emotional disturbance, the person holds a set of irrational beliefs about the inferences that she makes. In this context, a person will not feel ashamed about (a) falling short of her ideal, (b) letting down her reference group, (c) being let down by a member of her reference group and/or (d) others evaluating her negatively without holding irrational beliefs about these inferences.

So let me discuss which irrational beliefs are at the root of shame. As you will see, they take the form of a rigid demand and a self-depreciation belief about the four shame-related inferences discussed above. In the following sections I will outline the general irrational belief and illustrate it with a specific example.

Shame about falling short of an ideal

In general, in order to feel ashamed about falling short of an ideal, the person needs to hold a rigid demand about such a falling short (e.g. 'I must not fall short of my ideal') and a self-depreciation about her shortfall (e.g. '. . . and because I have fallen short, I am an inadequate person'). For example, Robert's ideal was to handle matters without showing anger. One day at work he lost his temper in front of his work colleagues. He felt ashamed about his shortfall by holding and practising the following shame-based irrational belief: 'I must not lose my temper in public and because I did, I am an inadequate person.'

Shame about letting down a reference group

In general, when a person feels ashamed about letting down her reference group, she holds a rigid demand about such a letting down (e.g. 'I must not let my reference group down') and a consequent self-depreciation belief (e.g. '. . . and because I have let them down, I am a shameful person'). For example, Petra belongs to a gang whose code of honour is always to support one another no matter what. Let's suppose further that Petra breaks that code by failing to support another gang member, thus letting down the gang. In order to make herself feel ashamed about her behaviour, she needs to hold and practise the following shame-based irrational belief: 'I absolutely should not have betrayed my fellow gang member and because I did, I am a shameful person.'

Shame about being let down by a member of her reference group

When a person feels ashamed about being let down by her reference group, she holds a rigid demand about such a let down (e.g. 'A member of my reference group must not let me and the group down') and a self-depreciation belief about this situation (e.g. '. . . and because they have let us down, it proves that we are inadequate'). For example, one of Adele's reference group that she holds dear considers crying in public to be a 'let down'. One day,

Fred, a member of Adele's reference group, cried in front of others: she viewed this as Fred letting her reference group down. Adele felt ashamed of Fred's 'let down' behaviour because she held the following shame-based irrational belief: 'Fred absolutely should not have broken down in tears in front of other people and because he did it proves that we are all (in our reference group) inadequate, weak, spineless individuals.'

Shame when being judged negatively in a shame-related context

When a person feels ashamed when others judge her negatively in a shame-related context (and again what is important here is that the person thinks that they are judging her rather than the facts of the situation), she once again holds a rigid demand about such a negative judgement (e.g. 'Others must not judge me negatively) and a self-depreciation belief about this judgement (e.g. '. . . and because they have judged me negatively, it proves that I am inadequate'). For example, Michael spoke up in a social context and mentioned something that was a taboo in that group. Michael thought that those present turned away from him in disgust. He felt ashamed about this negative judgement because he held the following shame-based irrational belief: 'This group absolutely should not have turned away from me in disgust and because they did, it proves that I am inadequate.'

The major shame-based negative self-judgements

I have made it clear in this section that at the core of shame a person holds shame-based irrational beliefs. I have stressed that these irrational beliefs have two major components: a rigid demand and a self-depreciation belief. A rigid demand is straightforward. It is absolute and comes in the form of a 'must', 'absolutely should', 'have to', 'got to', amongst others. Self-depreciation beliefs in shame are more varied, and in this section I will outline the major shame-based negative self-judgements. Before I list these self-depreciation beliefs, it is worth remembering that a self-depreciation belief involves a person making a global negative judgement about her entire self. The person is not just rating a part of herself, she is rating the whole of herself.

'I am defective'

People who feel ashamed often say: 'There is something wrong with me.' They don't mean that they are a fallible human being who may be defective in some respect. Rather, they mean that they are defective as a whole. In expressing this view, one of my clients said: 'If I was a car, the garage would say that I was beyond repair and should be scrapped.' In this context, when a person feels ashamed, she focuses on an aspect of herself that is negative and could do with improvement and then overgeneralises from this to the whole of her 'self'. In essence, the person believes: 'Because this part of me is defective, then I am defective.' As you will see, this process of overgeneralising from a part of oneself to the whole of oneself is common to all shame-based negative self-judgements.

'I am insignificant'

Sometimes when people feel ashamed they say that they 'feel small'. Behind this 'feeling' is the self-depreciation belief 'I am insignificant' and if a person holds this belief it is often in response to a situation where she has inferred, rightly or wrongly, that another person has belittled her in public. Here the person judges herself in the same way as she thinks the other person has judged her. It is as if the person thinks: 'I am who I think you say I am.'

'I am not good enough'

As I have already stated, people often feel ashamed when they fall short of their ideal. As I noted when discussing the 'I am defective' shame-based self-depreciation belief, people experiencing shame often make the part–whole error. This is also true when the content of the self-depreciation belief is 'I am not good enough.' Here, begin by noting that the person has failed to measure up to her ideal in some way. In this *part* of her life, the person may be correct in saying that she is not good enough *in this* respect, meaning that has not yet reached a certain standard. Then she makes a logical error in overgeneralising from that aspect to her entire self. For example: 'Because I am not good enough at public speaking, I am not good enough as a person.'

'I am weak/pathetic'

Listening to the self-evaluations that people who experience much shame in their lives make reveals that they often refer to themselves as being weak or pathetic. Thus, one of the ideals that such people demand that they must achieve is some sort of 'strength', either physical or mental. The latter particularly is prominent in shame. Thus, when a person feels ashamed in this area, she focuses on some aspect of her life where she is not as strong as she believes she absolutely should be. Then she globally rates herself as weak or pathetic. For example, Norma considers that it is weak to cry in public. One day, she cried in front of other people and felt ashamed about doing so. She felt ashamed about this weak display because she held the following irrational belief: 'I must not cry in public and because I did, I am a pathetic weak person.'

'I am disgusting'

The final way that a person can make herself feel ashamed is to view herself as a disgusting person. A frequent focus for a person's self-disgust is her (in this case) body. Christina had what she considered to be fat thighs. She made herself ashamed about her thighs first by making the following demand: 'My thighs absolutely should not be fat' and then by rating herself as disgusting: 'Because my thighs look disgusting, I am disgusting.' A person can apply this process to any aspect of her body that she particularly dislikes.

How a person can make herself feel ashamed by evaluating herself according to what happened to her

When a person feels ashamed about what has happened to her, she first demands that what happened absolutely should not have happened to her and then she overgeneralises the negative rating that she makes about the event to her entire self. Thus, Ruth was ridiculed in public by an acquaintance. She believed first that this absolutely should not have happened to her and then told herself that this ridicule proves that she is a stupid, shameful person.

Unconditional shame

So far, I have discussed how a person makes herself conditionally ashamed, which means that she feels ashamed when one or more of the following conditions exist. When she thinks that she has:

- fallen short of her ideal
- let down her reference group

- been let down by a member of her reference group
- been evaluated negatively by others.

Some people, however, think they are insignificant, defective or disgusting etc. because they are alive or because of who they are. In other words, their shame is unconditional. Consequently, it is unremitting and ever present.

Thinking that stems from shame-based irrational beliefs

When a person holds a shame-based irrational belief about thinking that (a) she has fallen very short of her ideal; (b) she has let down her reference group; (c) she has been let down by a member of her reference group and (d) others are judging her negatively, this belief will influence the way that she subsequently thinks. This thinking is characterised by exaggeration, overestimation of negative consequences and failure to appreciate that there may be a variety of responses to one's behaviour.

For example, Theo made himself feel ashamed about saying something stupid in front of a group of people.

Overestimating the 'shamefulness' of one's behaviour

Theo thought that what he said was very stupid (rather than moderately or mildly stupid).

Overestimating the extent to which others will notice one's 'shameful' behaviour

Theo thought that everyone present took notice of what he said.

Overestimating the likelihood that others will regard one's behaviour as 'shameful'

Theo thought that it was highly likely that everyone present thought that what he said was stupid.

Overestimating the extent to which others will regard one's behaviour as 'shameful'

Theo thought that those present regarded his behaviour as very stupid (rather than moderately or mildly stupid).

Overestimating the length of time that others will remember one's 'shameful' behaviour

Theo thought that those present would remember what he said for a very long time.

Overestimating the likelihood that others will regard one as 'shameful'

Theo thought that it was highly likely that those present considered that he (rather than just his behaviour) was stupid.

Overestimating the extent to which others will regard one as 'shameful'

Theo thought that those present regarded him as very stupid (rather than mildly or moderately stupid).

Overestimating the length of time that others will regard one as 'shameful'

Theo thought that those present would consider him stupid for a very long time.

Overestimating the likelihood that those observing will tell others about one

Theo thought that it was highly likely that those present would tell others about what he said.

Exaggerating what those observing will tell others about one

Theo thought that those present would tell others what a very stupid person he was.

Exaggerating the extent to which others will ridicule one

Theo thought that those present would ridicule him very badly.

Exaggerating the extent to which others will exclude one

Theo thought that those present would exclude him and not want anything to do with him in the future.

It is important to bear in mind that while all the above thinking consequences of shame-based irrational beliefs are possible, the extent to which they are likely to occur is grossly exaggerated by the person.

Behaviour that stems from shame-based irrational beliefs

When a person holds shame-based irrational beliefs, she will tend to act in certain ways. Many of these behaviours are both an expression of shame and an attempt by the person to avoid the pain of these feelings. The main point to note is that these behaviours both stem from the person's shame-based irrational beliefs and, when she engages in them, help to strengthen her conviction in these beliefs. As such, engaging in the following shame-based behaviours renders the person more vulnerable to experiencing shame.

Physically withdrawing from others

When a person feels ashamed, she will experience a strong tendency to physically withdraw from the people who she thinks have witnessed her 'shameful' behaviour and are evaluating her negatively for it. When the person gives in to this tendency and actually withdraws from these people, she will immediately experience a sense of relief. However, this will be short-lived and withdrawing in this way will result in the person experiencing shame in the future because she has strengthened her shame-based irrational beliefs. By physically withdrawing from others after revealing a weakness to them, for example, the person is in effect saying: 'If I remain in the presence of these people after acting weakly in front of them, I will see them look down on me and this will mean that I am a weak person for acting weakly, which I absolutely should not have done. Therefore I will leave.'

Looking away from others

When a person experiences shame in the presence of others, she will tend to look down and away from their gaze. Doing so will result in the person unwittingly strengthening her shame-based irrational beliefs. Averting her gaze from others is a form of psychological withdrawal. It strengthens shame-based irrational beliefs in a way similar to physically withdrawing from others. By looking away from others, after revealing a weakness to them, for example, the person is in effect saying: 'If I look at these people after acting weakly in front of them, I will see them look down on me and this will mean that I am a weak person for acting weakly, which I absolutely should not have done. Therefore I will avoid their gaze.'

Isolating oneself from others

Once a person feels ashamed and perhaps after she has physically withdrawn from the shame-related situation, she will tend to perpetuate her shame-based irrational belief by isolating herself from others. For example, when Christina did this, she was in effect saying: 'Because I am a disgusting person for revealing my fat thighs in public, I'll avoid other people in case they see them.'

Denying responsibility for one's actions

When a person has made herself feel ashamed, she will be tempted to get rid of these feelings of shame by denying responsibility for her actions. Once again, doing so will perpetuate her shame-based irrational beliefs and make it more likely that she will feel shame in the future. Let me give you an example. Sandra insulted her boss's husband at the works Christmas party. She began to feel ashamed because she believed that she showed herself to be stupid. To get rid of these feelings, she quickly denied responsibility for her actions by blaming them on the medication that she claimed to be taking (but in reality wasn't).

Concealing verbally and physically

Shame and concealment often go together. A person can hide when she feels ashamed and she can hide in order to prevent herself from feeling ashamed. Either way, when a person acts in a concealing manner she reinforces her shame-based irrational beliefs.

When a person uses verbal concealment, she decides to say very little about herself to others. She tends to be quite superficial in her conversations with others and certainly does not say anything that might be taken as controversial by those present. The reason why the person conceals is to avoid feeling ashamed. It is as if she is saying to herself: 'I will not reveal anything that could be construed as controversial about myself because if I do others may look down on me and I must not be disapproved by others. If this happens it proves that I am inadequate.'

When concealment is physical, the person hides aspects of her body from others because she feels ashamed of herself for having such aspects. For example, Christina's concealment of her thighs was underpinned by a shame-creating irrational belief: 'Others must not see how fat my thighs are, and if they do they will think that I am disgusting and they would be right. I am disgusting for having my fat thighs. Therefore, I will hide them from public view.'

Overcompensating for one's feelings of shame

Another way in which a person unwittingly perpetuates her shame-creating irrational beliefs, and thus makes it more likely that she feels shame, is for that person to act in a way that overcompensates for her shame. For example, Warren, who feels ashamed of being small and of weak stature, overcompensates for this by showing everyone how physically strong he is.

Thus, when a person overcompensates for her feelings of shame, she tends to do the very opposite of what she feels ashamed about.

People develop and rehearse general shame-based irrational beliefs

General shame-based irrational beliefs are irrational beliefs that a person holds in many theme-related situations that result in her experiencing shame in these situations. Developing and rehearsing such beliefs will lead her to experience shame in many different situations. She will do this mainly because she becomes skilled at inferring, for example, that she has fallen short of her ideal and that other people will evaluate her negatively for this even when there is scant supporting evidence for the latter.

Let me show you how this works. First, the person develops general shame-based irrational beliefs, such as: 'I must always live up to my ideals and if I don't, then I am inadequate' and 'Other people must not disapprove of me and if they do, it proves that I am inadequate.' She then rehearses these beliefs until she firmly believes them and brings them to relevant situations where it is possible that (a) she will not live up to her ideal and that (b) others will disapprove of her. Then, because she cannot convince herself that she will live up to her ideal and that she will not be disapproved of, she thinks that she has fallen short of her ideal (in a big way) and that people will disapprove of her for this. Having created these shame-based inferences, she develops and holds specific versions of these general shame-based irrational beliefs about these inferences and thereby makes herself feel ashamed in these specific situations.

Let me give you a concrete example. Stephen developed the following two general shame-based irrational beliefs: 'I must never lose my temper in public and if I do, I am a weak person' and 'Others must approve of me and if they don't, I am inadequate.' He took these two beliefs to a specific situation where a waiter in a restaurant brought him the wrong dish and he snapped at the waiter very briefly. Stephen's two general shame-based irrational beliefs led him to make the following inferences about this event: (a) 'I lost my temper with the waiter' (because of his first general shame-based irrational belief he inferred that snapping briefly at the waiter was tantamount to losing his temper with him) and (b) 'Others witnessing this disapproved of me for losing my temper with the waiter' (because of his second general shame-based irrational belief he inferred that because those present would not approve of him for this incident, therefore they would disapprove of him for it). Stephen's belief did not permit him to consider that they might think he was justified in his behaviour or that they did not take any notice or that they might briefly disapprove of his behaviour but still basically approve of him.

Once Stephen created his inferences, he made himself feel ashamed about them by holding specific versions of his general shame-inducing irrational beliefs. Thus 'I lost my temper with the waiter and incurred the disapproval of those present. I absolutely should not have done either of these things and because I did, I am a weak, inadequate person.'

Then, Stephen thought and acted in ways that were consistent with his shame-based irrational beliefs, which had the effect of strengthening his conviction in these beliefs.

People develop and rehearse a view of the world founded on shame-based irrational beliefs

I have said that people develop ideas about the world as it relates to them and some of these 'world views' render them vulnerable to particular unhealthy negative emotions. These world views that render a person vulnerable to shame do so because they make it very easy for her to make shame-related inferences. Then, as I have shown earlier in the chapter, the person makes herself feel ashamed about these inferences with the appropriate irrational beliefs. Here is an illustrative list of shame-related world views that a person may develop and the inferences that they spawn.

World view: There is always the danger that I will not achieve my ideal standards.
Inference: I have not reached my ideal and am showing a weakness.

World view: Social situations are dangerous because I may be exposed at any moment.
Inference: If I reveal a weakness, no matter how small, people will easily spot this.

World view: Social situations are dangerous because other people will judge me negatively if I put a foot wrong.
Inference: If I reveal a weakness, people will judge me negatively.

Further reading

Academic

Tangney, J.P. & Dearing, R.L. (2002). *Shame and guilt.* New York: Guilford.

Self-help

Dryden, W. (1997). *Overcoming shame.* London: Sheldon.

In the next chapter, I will consider the emotion of guilt. Guilt is often linked with shame and there are certainly some similarities between the two emotions. However, there are also major differences between the two, as you will see.

Chapter 4

Understanding guilt

Before I discuss guilt, a word on terminology. I make the distinction between being guilty and feeling guilty. By *being guilty*, I refer to the person taking responsibility for doing something wrong, for failing to do the right thing or for harming or hurting someone. By *feeling guilty*, I mean the emotion that a person experiences when she blames or condemns herself for one or more of the above. Because it is based on unhealthy irrational beliefs and generally has negative consequences, guilt is a disturbed negative emotion. A feeling of remorse is a healthy response to doing wrong, for example, because it is based on responsibility without self-blame and generally has healthy consequences.

How a person makes herself feel guilty: general steps

In order for a person to feel guilty and stay feeling guilty, the person tends to do the following:

1   She makes a guilt-related inference.
2   She brings guilt-based irrational beliefs to that inference.
3   She thinks in ways that are consistent with the above irrational beliefs.
4   She acts in ways that are consistent with these irrational beliefs.
5   She rehearses a general version of her specific guilt-based irrational beliefs so that she easily makes guilt-based inferences about what is generally going on in her life as well as what she is not doing.
6   She develops and rehearses a guilt-based world view.

I will deal with these issues one at a time.

Guilt-related inferences

To feel guilty, a person needs to make one or more inferences about what is going on in her life. Once again these inferences neither have to reflect accurately what the person has done (or not done) or the outcome of her behaviour (or lack of behaviour). The important point is that the person has to believe that they are true. Here is a list of common guilt-related inferences:

'I have broken my moral or ethical code'

Here are some suggestions of what a person can focus on under this heading to begin the guilt experience:

- Badmouthing one of her friends to another friend.
- Cheating on her partner.
- Making racist remarks.

'I have failed to live up to my moral or ethical code'

For example:

- Failing to help someone who required assistance.
- Not praying every day.
- Not giving to charity.

'I have harmed or hurt the feelings of others'

For example:

- Forgetting her mother's birthday with the result that her mother feels hurt.
- Telling her child off so that he/she cries.
- Getting someone into trouble at work.

The person holds and rehearses irrational beliefs about her guilt-related inference

Once again, I want to stress that it is the person's inferences that make the person feel disturbed, and at the heart of her disturbance is a set of irrational beliefs about the inferences that she makes. In this context, the person will not feel guilty about (a) breaking her moral or ethical code, (b) not living up to her moral or ethical code or (c) harming someone or hurting their feelings without holding irrational beliefs about these inferences.

So let me discuss the irrational beliefs that are at the root of guilt. As with shame, they take the form of a rigid demand and a self-depreciation belief about the three guilt-related inferences that I discussed above. I will outline the general irrational belief and illustrate it with a specific example.

Guilt about breaking a moral or ethical code

In general, in order to feel guilty about breaking a moral or ethical code, the person needs to hold a rigid demand about such a code violation (e.g. 'I must not break my moral or ethical code') and a self-depreciation about it (e.g. '. . . and because I have broken it, I am a bad person'). For example, one of Fiona's moral rules was that it is wrong to let her friends down. On one occasion, she was faced with a choice of getting a free holiday and letting down a friend or supporting her friend and missing out on the holiday. On an impulse she decided to go for the free holiday, which meant that she let down her friend. Fiona made herself guilty about her code violation by holding and practising the following guilt-based irrational belief: 'I absolutely should not have let down my friend and because I did, I am a bad person.'

Guilt about not living up to a moral or ethical code

The difference between this situation and the above is that in the above the person has committed a sin (known as the sin of commission), i.e. she has done the wrong thing. Here, the person has failed to do the right thing (known as the sin of omission). In general, in order to feel guilty about failing to live up to a moral or ethical code, the person again tends to hold a rigid demand about such a failure (e.g. 'I must live up to my moral or ethical code') and a consequent self-depreciation belief (e.g. '. . . and because I have not, I am a bad person'). For example, Roger thinks that going to the aid of someone is the right thing to do. One night Roger saw someone being attacked, but instead of going to the person's aid, he turned and walked away from the incident. From his frame of reference, he failed to live up to his ethical code. To feel guilty about his behaviour, Roger brought to the incident the following guilt-based irrational belief: 'I absolutely should have gone to the aid of that person and because I didn't, I am a bad person.'

Guilt about harming or hurting the feelings of someone else

In general, in order to feel guilty about harming or hurting the feelings of someone else, a person tends to hold a rigid demand about her role in this situation (e.g. 'I absolutely should not harm or hurt someone') and a self-depreciation about her role (e.g. '. . . and because I did, I am a bad person'). For example, Stephanie wanted to visit her parents over Easter, while her partner wanted to visit his in a different part of the country. One way for Stephanie to feel guilty about this situation is for her to think 'My partner is upset and I am the cause', and then to hold the following guilt-based irrational belief. 'I upset him, which I must not do and this proves what a bad, selfish person I am.' Another way for Stephanie to practise this guilt-based irrational belief in this situation, but this time without feeling guilty (I call this a way of rehearsing emotional disturbance without feeling it) is for her to go along with her partner's wishes. She would do so because (a) she thinks that he would be upset about not seeing his parents and more importantly (b) she would make herself feel guilty about this because she would hold the following guilt-producing irrational belief: 'If I went to see his parents, I know that he would be upset and I would be the cause of this. I must not upset my partner and I am a bad, selfish person if I do.'

The major guilt-based negative self-judgements

As I have shown, when a person feels guilt, the essence of this emotion is the person holding and practising guilt-based irrational beliefs. Moreover I have stressed that these irrational beliefs have two major components: a rigid demand and a self-depreciation belief. A rigid demand, as we have seen, is relatively straight-forward. It is absolute and comes in the form of a 'must', 'abso-lutely should', 'have to', 'got to', amongst others. Self-depreciation beliefs in guilt are a little more varied (although not as varied as in shame) and here I will outline the major guilt-based negative self-judgements.

Before I list these self-depreciation beliefs, remember that a self-depreciation belief involves a person making a global negative judgement about her entire self. She is not rating a part of herself, she is rating the whole of her 'self'.

'I am bad'

The main form of self-depreciation in guilt is 'I am bad.' This is sometimes expressed as 'I am a bad person', 'I am rotten' or 'I am a rotten person.' The hallmark of this form of self-depreciation at the point when a person is experiencing guilt is that her entire 'self' is morally corrupt. Most of the time the person thinks this way after she has (a) broken her moral code; (b) failed to live up to her moral code or (c) harmed or hurt someone's feelings as I have discussed above. And when the person does so, she is making the part–whole error: evaluating her entire self on the basis of one of its parts. In simple terms, she jumps from 'it's bad' to 'I'm bad.' For example:

'Because I stole stationery from my place of work, I am a bad person.'

'Because I failed to go to the help of that person being attacked I am bad.'

'Because I hurt my sister's feelings by saying that I didn't like her new dress, I am a rotten person.'

This process of overgeneralising from a part of a person to the whole of her is common to virtually all guilt-based negative self-judgements.

'I am less good than I would have been if . . .'

Although a person may not condemn herself, she may still make herself feel guilty (although not as guilty as when she does condemn herself) by evaluating herself as less good than she would be if she hadn't done the wrong thing, had done the right thing or hadn't caused harm or hurt to others. For example, if Roger failed to live up to his moral/ethical code by not going to the aid of another person needing help, he can still make himself feel guilty by believing: 'I absolutely should have helped that person and since I didn't, I am less good than I would have been if I had helped him.'

'I am selfish'

One of the characteristics of people who experience chronic guilt (i.e. they feel guilty often and across different situations) is that in reality they tend to be selfless and put the interests of others before their own. When they even think of putting their own healthy interests before the interests of others they feel guilty and back down because they believe: 'I must make sure that others are catered for before I go for what I want and if I put myself before others, then I am a selfish person.'

The following vignette illustrates this dynamic. Helen was a 40-year-old, single woman who was the principal carer for her aging mother with whom she lived. Helen regularly put her mother's interests before her own, with the result that she rarely went out and had virtually no social life. However, she did have two old school friends who were very loyal to her. These friends badgered Helen incessantly to allow them to take her out to celebrate her 40th birthday, even arranging for a professional carer to look after her mother. Eventually, albeit reluctantly, Helen agreed to go after obsessively checking with her mother that she didn't mind. However, just before going into the posh restaurant that her friends had booked for the celebration, Helen made herself feel severely guilty and made her apologies before rushing home to her mother. Helen did this because she held the following belief: 'I must not enjoy myself when I know that my mother is not enjoying herself. Because I am putting my pleasure before my mother's feelings I am a selfish person.'

People like Helen shuttle between two position in their mind: selflessness and selfishness. When a person does this, she is basically saying that either she puts other people's interests before her own or she is a selfish person. What often fuels this belief is the person's idea that she is unimportant and the only way that she can gain a sense of importance is by ensuring that she helps others achieve their goals or ensures that they don't get upset. Such an idea results in the person becoming highly susceptible to others manipulating her through guilt. Thus, Helen's mother successfully manipulated Helen by saying things like: 'Don't worry about me dear, I'll be alright', while giving her a pained expression. What this really meant, as Helen fully realised, was: 'I'll be upset if you go out and it will be all your fault.'

When an individual believes that she is a selfish person, she is doing three things:

– She acknowledges that her behaviour is selfish. It often isn't, but the person infers that it is.
– She assumes that because she has acted selfishly she scores highly on the trait known as 'selfishness'.
– She is using that trait description to define herself. It is as if she is saying:
'Because I have acted selfishly, I have selfishness and I am therefore a selfish person.' Once the person habitually makes this 'behaviour → trait → self' translation process, she skips the middle step and defines her 'self' on the basis of her behaviour [behaviour → self], e.g. 'Because I acted selfishly, I am a selfish person.

Finally, when an individual believes that she is a selfish person, most of the time she is implying (although she does not make explicit) that she is a bad person or certainly less good than she would be if she scored highly on selflessness or acted selflessly.

'I don't deserve good things to happen to me. I only deserve bad things . . .'

Another way that a person can make herself feel unhealthily guilty is to consider herself undeserving of good things, but deserving of bad. This is a more subtle form of self-depreciation and thus more difficult to identify. But if a person feels guilty and denies the other forms of guilt-based self-depreciation, then she may well resonate with this one.

Unconditional guilt

So far, I have discussed how a person makes herself conditionally guilty, which means that she feels guilty when one or more of the following conditions are in place. When the person thinks that she has:

- broken her moral code
- failed to live up to her moral code
- harmed or hurt someone's feelings.

Some people, however, think they are bad people because they are alive, or because of who they are. In other words, their guilt is unconditional. Consequently, like unconditional shame, it is unremitting and ever present.

Thinking that stems from guilt-based irrational beliefs

When a person holds a guilt-based irrational belief about thinking that (a) she has broken her moral code; (b) she has failed to do the right thing and/or (c) she has caused harm or hurt to others, this belief will influence the way that she subsequently thinks, as discussed below.

Exaggerating the badness of one's behaviour

Once a person has made herself feel guilty about her 'sin', she tends to think about what she did in exaggerated ways. In particular, she may think that her actions are much worse than when she first focused on them. Thus, Mary first made herself feel guilty about hurting her parents' feelings by refusing to do their shopping for them. She then exaggerated this by showing herself that her actions were despicably selfish. Having exaggerated the badness of her behaviour in this way, Mary then brought a further guilt-inducing irrational belief to this exaggeration, thus making herself even more guilty.

Exaggerating the negative consequences of one's behaviour and minimising its positive consequences

Once a person has made herself feel guilty about her 'sin', she exaggerates the negative consequences of her behaviour and minimises its positive consequences. Thus, Simon made himself feel guilty about stealing stationery from work. Having done so, he thought that he was bound to get caught and when he did, he would be fired and find it difficult to get another job (exaggerating the negative consequences of his behaviour). He edited out what he could productively learn from this episode (i.e. that he stole it because he thought he needed it and that he could challenge the belief that he must have what he wants, minimising the positive consequences of his behaviour).

Assuming more personal responsibility for what happened and assigning less responsibility to others than the situation warrants

Once a person has made herself feel guilty and she looks back on her 'sin' and all the factors involved, she tends to assume far more responsibility than the situation warrants and assigns far less responsibility to relevant others. She thinks that it is all her fault.

In addition, the person keeps her feelings of guilt alive by editing out of the picture the responsibility that others have for their own feelings. She does this when she thinks that she can hurt other people's feelings. Actually, she cannot hurt their feelings. She can treat people badly, harm them physically or materially, but she can't hurt their feelings since they have the choice whether or not to disturb themselves or not about the person's behaviour towards them.

Engaging in 'if only' thinking

'If only' thinking serves to perpetuate guilt after the person has begun to experience this emotion. Harold made, in good faith, a business decision that unfortunately did not work out, with the result that he had to sack two of his employees to ensure that his company continued trading. He made himself feel guilty by believing that he absolutely should not have acted in a way that had such bad consequences and that he is a bad person because he did. Harold unwittingly maintained his guilt feelings by showing himself that if only he hadn't acted in that way, then he would not have had to sack his two employees. This reinforces Harold's idea that he alone was responsible for sacking his employees. Of course, it may be true that if Harold hadn't made the decision, then the two employees would not have lost their jobs. However, it could equally be true that if Harold hadn't made the decision, then other bad things would have happened.

However, under the influence of his guilt, Harold thought that this bad outcome would not have happened if he hadn't made the decision, and that a good outcome would have happened if he had made a different decision. In doing so, he gave himself a double dose of guilt. First, he made himself feel guilty for taking sole responsibility for the bad outcome ('I am a bad person because I made a decision that resulted in me having to sack two of my employees. I absolutely should not have made such a bad decision'). Second, he made himself feel guilty for not making a different, more effective decision ('If only I made that other investment that I was considering at the time, then I would not have had to lay off my two employees and things would have flourished. I am a bad person for not making the right decision as I absolutely should have done').

Judging what one did with the benefit of hindsight only

One of the things that people who don't make themselves feel unhealthily guilty do is to look back at their 'sin' from the perspective of when they took action. Thus, they are able to say: 'Yes, I now see that I broke my moral code, but I was so fixated on getting what I wanted, it did not occur to me that I was breaking my moral code. What I have learned from this situation is that I need to deal with my tendency to become fixated so that I can be more aware of the implications of my behaviour.' In contrast, a person who often experiences guilt does not do this. Rather, she only judges her behaviour from the benefit of hindsight (e.g. 'I could have foreseen what I was going to do and therefore I absolutely should have done so' or 'I now see that it would have been better to do "x" rather than "y", therefore I absolutely should have done "y"'). As you can see, hindsight thinking stems from absolute thinking and together they make a very powerful guilt-inducing cocktail. In short, the person believes: 'Because I could have done things differently, I absolutely should have done things differently.'

Not taking into account mitigating factors or showing oneself compassion

Once the person has made herself feel guilty she will tend to discount what might be called mitigating factors, i.e. genuine reasons that may help the person take an understanding, compassionate view of her 'sin'. Colloquially, this is called being hard on oneself! If the person believes that she absolutely should not have broken her moral code, such rigidity precludes her from understanding aspects of the situation that may have prompted her to act as she did. This is why I say that guilt and the rigid beliefs that it is based on are the enemies of understanding.

Failing to appreciate the complexity of the situation

When a person does something wrong, for example, her behaviour is most accurately viewed from a complex perspective. Thus, when Roxanne let down her friend, she faced a choice between letting down her friend and letting down her parents. She decided to let down her friend because she thought that it was the lesser of the two evils. Because she held the belief: 'I must not let down people I care about', she looked at this situation in 'black and white' terms. She concluded: 'letting down my friend was just plain wrong and that's the end of it. It cannot be justified'.

Thinking that one will receive due retribution for one's behaviour

As I have already discussed, when a person makes herself feel guilty one of the guilt-inducing irrational beliefs that she holds is that she is a bad person. When she thinks that she is a bad person, this belief encourages her to think that bad things will happen to her because she thinks that she deserves retribution for being a bad person. In short, she believes that bad things happen to bad people because they deserve punishment.

Behaviour that stems from guilt-based irrational beliefs

When a person holds guilt-based irrational beliefs, she will tend to act in certain ways. Once again, you will note that many of these behaviours are both an expression of guilt and an attempt by the person to avoid the pain of these feelings. The main point to note is that these behaviours both stem from the person's guilt-based irrational beliefs and, when she engages in them, they help to strengthen her conviction in these beliefs. As such, engaging in guilt-based behaviours renders the person more vulnerable to experiencing guilt.

Confessing regardless of the consequences

Some say that confession is good for the soul and this may be the case if a person thinks carefully about the consequences of her confession and judges that it will do her more good than harm. However, the person who is prone to guilt believes that she has to confess her 'sin' to the people involved regardless of the consequences. In doing so, she will strengthen her guilt-based irrational belief: 'I am a bad person and I must unburden myself to become good again.' Of course, confession (outside a religious context) doesn't lead the person to become good again and there is a very good chance that the consequences of her confession will be harmful to her and the other(s) involved. This latter point demonstrates how the person can give herself a double dose of guilt: 'I am a bad person for doing what I did in the first place and a bad person for upsetting the other(s) by confessing my sin in the second place.' So, thoughtless confession will lead the person further down the guilt road.

Begging for forgiveness

Another way that a person unwittingly strengthens her guilt-based irrational beliefs is to beg for forgiveness from the other person that she has wronged, harmed or hurt. In begging rather than asking for forgiveness the person deepens her conviction that she is a bad despicable creature who can only be raised up if the other person forgives her. If she is not, she remains a bad person in her mind. If she is forgiven, she feels better temporarily, but since her conviction in her badness remains unchecked, she needs frequent reassurance that the other has still forgiven her. She thus frequently seeks reassurance from this other person that she is still forgiven.

Promising unrealistically not to 'sin' again

After the person has wronged, harmed or hurt someone and has made herself feel guilty about doing so, one way that the person attempts to make herself feel better in the short term is to promise the other person that she will not 'sin' again. If the other person accepts her promise, she will feel mightily relieved, but in all probability she won't take steps to put her promise into practice by seeking help to address the factors that led her to 'sin' in the first place. Consequently, she will probably 'sin' again if she encounters these factors and, if she does, she will probably make herself feel guilty for her behaviour all over again. On the other hand, if the other person does not accept her promise, she will not gain this short-term relief and will continue to make herself feel guilty about her 'sin'.

Depriving oneself

When a person has made herself feel guilty, she tends to think that she doesn't deserve any good things in life. To reinforce this view, she deprives herself of the good things in life. She may not see her friends, for example, and may not engage in any pleasurable activities. In doing so, she implicitly rehearses the view that the reason she is depriving herself is that as a person she does not deserve such pleasure because of her 'sin'.

Punishing oneself

A more extreme version of depriving oneself is punishing oneself. Here, the person is not just saying that she does not deserve good things in her life, she is also saying that she deserves bad things in her life. Consequently, the person tends to actively seek out such bad things. For example, she may seek out and spend time with people who actively dislike her or she may wish to engage in tasks that she actively dislikes. In doing so, she is acting on the belief that because of her 'sin' she deserves to be treated badly by people who dislike her and she is only fit to engage in tasks she hates.

Doing penance

When a person punishes herself for her 'sin', she is, in effect, saying that because she is bad she deserves to experience bad things. However, when a person does penance for her 'sin' (e.g. deliberately undertaking something onerous), she is saying that she can redeem herself from her badness by her penance. In doing so, she still holds and unwittingly strengthens the belief that she is a bad person for her 'sin'.

Disclaiming responsibility

When a person has done something wrong, failed to do the right thing or has caused harm or hurt to someone and she holds a guilt-inducing irrational belief about her 'sin', she will *tend to* make herself guilty. I say 'tend to' here because the person can still stop herself from feeling guilty before guilt takes a hold. She can do this by disclaiming responsibility for her actions. Basically, she can do this in two ways. First, she can place the responsibility on some external factor. This might be another person (e.g. 'Yes, I did let you down, but it was my brother's fault. He made me do it') or some aspect of the environment (e.g. 'I would have helped you out, but the train was delayed'). Second, she can place the responsibility on some internal factor like illness or medication (e.g. 'I don't know what came over me. It must have been the medication I am on'). While the person will not actually experience feelings of guilt if she disclaims responsibility in these ways, she is still rehearsing her guilt-inducing irrational beliefs, albeit implicitly. For example, when Mark tries to convince himself that the reason why he let down his friend was due to his brother, he is implicitly saying: 'If I acknowledge that I was responsible for letting the other person down, then I would be a bad person. Therefore, to stop blaming myself, I will blame someone else.'

Overcompensating for feelings of guilt

Another way of coping with feelings of guilt is to overcompensate for them. This involves the person doing the very opposite of what she feels guilty about. However, when the person does this it does result in strengthening her guilt-inducing irrational belief. Thus, Roberta believed that she is a bad person for having upset her friend. She overcompensated for her guilt feelings by going out of her way to be nice to people. She did that because she thought that the only way that she could get away from the belief that she is bad was by doing good. However, in doing so, she unwittingly strengthened the idea that her moral worth as a person is based on the way she treats others. This exemplifies the conditional philosophy of guilt: 'I am bad if I treat others badly. I am good if I treat others well.'

Trying to get reassurance from others, but failing to be reassured

After a person has made herself feel guilty for her 'sin', she may be tempted to ask people for reassurance that what she did wasn't wrong, that there was a good reason for what she did, or that she wasn't really responsible for her actions. It is likely that she will find plenty of people to give her such reassurance, but she won't stay reassured for long. Believing that she is a bad person for doing what she absolutely should not have done means that she is not reassurable even if an army of volunteers are recruited to reassure her. It will only take one person to say that what she did was wrong and her guilt-inducing irrational belief will lead her back to: 'But it was wrong' and from there 'Since it was wrong, I absolutely should not have done it, and because I did, I am a bad person.'

The same process happens when another person convinces her for the moment that there was good reason for what she did or that she wasn't really responsible for her actions. Here, as before, the person's guilt-inducing irrational belief will lead her to go back and say to herself: 'But there really wasn't a good reason for my behaviour' or 'But I am responsible for my actions.' When she does go back, she will then feel guilty because she will bring her guilt-inducing irrational belief to these inferences.

People develop and rehearse general guilt-based irrational beliefs

General guilt-based irrational beliefs are irrational beliefs that a person holds in many theme-related situations, which result in that person experiencing guilt in these situations. Developing and rehearsing such beliefs will lead the person to experience guilt in many different situations. She will do this mainly because she becomes practised at inferring, for example, that she has broken her moral or ethical code, failed to live up to her moral or ethical code or caused harm or hurt to relevant others.

Let me show you how this works. First, the person develops general guilt-based irrational beliefs such as: 'I must never cause hurt or harm to those that I care about and if I do, then this proves that I am a bad person.' She then rehearses these beliefs until she firmly believes them and brings them to relevant situations where it is possible that she caused harm or hurt to relevant others. Then, because she cannot convince herself that she will not harm or hurt the other person, she will tend to think that she has harmed or hurt that person. Having created this guilt-based inference, she develops and holds a specific version of this general guilt-based irrational belief and thereby makes herself feel guilty in this specific situation.

Let me give you a concrete example. Leona developed the following general guilt-based irrational belief: 'I must not upset my mother and if I do, I am a bad person.' She took this belief to a specific situation where her mother asked her over for dinner and she said 'no' because she was going out with a friend that night. She explained this to her mother, but was not sure of her mother's reaction. Her general guilt-based irrational belief led her to infer that she upset her mother. It as if she reasoned: 'Because I can't convince myself that I didn't upset my mother, therefore I did.' Her belief did not allow her to think that her mother was probably OK with her not going to dinner.

Once Leona created her inference, she made herself feel guilty about it by holding a specific version of her general guilt-inducing irrational belief. Thus 'I upset my mother by turning down her dinner invitation. I absolutely should not have upset my mother in this way and I am a bad person because I did.' Having made herself feel guilty in this way, Leona then thought and acted in ways that were consistent with her guilt-based irrational belief, which had the effect of strengthening this belief.

People develop and rehearse a view of the world founded on guilt-based irrational beliefs

I have mentioned several times now that people develop world views that render them vulnerable to particular unhealthy negative emotions. The world views that render a person vulnerable to guilt do so again because they make it very easy for her to make guilt-related inferences. Then, as I have shown you earlier in the chapter, the person makes herself feel guilty about these inferences with the appropriate irrational beliefs. Here is an illustrative list of guilt-related world views that a person may develop and the inferences that they spawn.

World view: Other people's desires are more important than mine.
Inference: If I put my desires first I am being selfish.

World view: I have responsibility for the hurt feelings of others.
Inference: If someone's feelings are hurt and I have been involved, then I have hurt that person's feelings.

World view: In the moral domain, I expect more of myself than I do of others.
Inference: There is no excuse for what I did.

Further reading

Academic

Tangney, J.P. & Dearing, R.L. (2002). *Shame and guilt.* New York: Guilford.

Self-help

Dryden, W. (1994). *Overcoming guilt.* London: Sheldon.

In the next chapter, I will help you to understand unhealthy anger.

Chapter 5

Understanding unhealthy anger

Unhealthy anger is a particularly destructive emotion. It normally has bad psychological and physical effects on the individual and it also sours relationships. Once again I will first outline the general steps that a person tends to take to make herself feel unhealthily angry before discussing each step in some detail.

Before I do so, let me discuss terminology again. Anger is an easily misunderstood emotion unless we distinguish between unhealthy and healthy anger. By *unhealthy anger* (towards another in this case), I mean a state where the person demands that the other person must or must not act in a certain way and where she condemns the other person for their actions. Her inclination is to attack the other person in some way and she thinks that they have malevolent intent towards her in their actions in the absence of substantiating evidence. By contrast, *healthy anger* is a state where the person prefers the other person to act or not act in a certain way, but does demand that her preference is met. She evaluates the other person's behaviour as bad, but does not condemn them for their actions. Her inclination is to confront the other person assertively without attacking them and she doesn't necessarily think that they have malevolent intent towards her in their behaviour unless it was clear that this was the case.

How a person makes herself unhealthily angry: general steps

The steps that a person takes to make herself unhealthily angry should be familiar to you by now since they are the same as I outlined in the previous chapters. Just to refresh your memory, here they are as applied to unhealthy anger.

1   The person makes an unhealthy anger-related inference.
2   She brings a set of unhealthy anger-based irrational beliefs to that inference.
3   She thinks in ways that are consistent with the above irrational beliefs.
4   She acts in ways that are consistent with these irrational beliefs.
5   She rehearses a general version of her specific unhealthy anger-based irrational beliefs so that she easily makes unhealthy anger-related inferences.
6   She develops and rehearses an unhealthy anger-based world view.

Now let me deal with these issues one at a time. As I do so, I will concentrate on how a person makes herself feel unhealthy anger towards others. What I say, however, can easily be generalised so that you can understand how the person makes herself feel unhealthily angry towards herself and towards life conditions.

Unhealthy anger-related inferences

To feel unhealthy anger, the person needs to make one or more inferences about what is going on in her life. Once again these inferences don't have to reflect accurately what happened. The important point is that the person has to believe that they are true. Here is a list of common unhealthy anger-related inferences:

Another person (or group of people) transgresses a socially agreed rule, a legal rule or one's own rule

There are socially agreed rules for behaviour, legal rules for behaviour and individuals have their own rules about the people they come into contact with. Here are some examples of others transgressing the above rules:

- Someone jumps a supermarket queue (person breaks socially agreed rule).
- Someone drives through a red light (person breaks legal rule).

- Someone turns up late for an appointment with an individual (person breaks individual's rule).

Being blocked or frustrated in her progress towards a goal

As humans we all have goals that we strive to achieve. Being blocked or frustrated in our pursuit towards our goals often serves as an activating event for unhealthy anger. Here are a few examples:

- Being stuck in a traffic jam.
- Another person blocking the person's promotion.
- Missing a train connection.

Injustice/unfairness

A person thinking that she has been treated unjustly or unfairly is a theme that often is found in descriptions of episodes of unhealthy anger. In addition, the person can make herself unhealthily angry about injustice or unfairness that has befallen others. Here are a few examples of each:

- The person being promised a raise if she works overtime but not receiving it, even though she kept her side of the bargain.
- Being prosecuted for a crime that the person did not commit.
- Another person being prosecuted for a crime that they did not commit.
- A child being shouted at unfairly by a parent.

Threat to self-esteem

As I will discuss later in this chapter, there is a distinction between unhealthy ego anger and unhealthy non-ego anger. In unhealthy ego anger, the person makes herself unhealthily angry about events that impinge on her self-esteem. Here are a number of such events:

- rejection
- being criticised
- being ridiculed.

Being treated with disrespect

Being treated with disrespect may be a stimulus for the person making herself unhealthily angry in both ego and non-ego domains.

The person holds and rehearses irrational beliefs about her unhealthy anger-related inference

When a person makes herself unhealthily angry, she often states or implies that what happened to her (or her inferences about what happened to her) made her unhealthily angry (e.g. 'missing the bus made me furious' or 'your criticism of me made me angry'). As you now know, the person is wrong about this. For it is not what happened to the person or her inferences about that which made her feel unhealthy anger, rather she felt unhealthy anger because of the irrational beliefs that she held about the inferences that she made. In this context, the person will not feel unhealthily angry about being frustrated, others transgressing her rules, being rejected or criticised, for example, without holding irrational beliefs about these inferences.

So let me discuss the irrational beliefs that are at the core of unhealthy anger.

Two types of unhealthy anger

Before I do so, I want to make an important distinction between two types of unhealthy anger: unhealthy ego anger and unhealthy non-ego anger. When a person makes herself unhealthily angry in the ego domain she is angry at someone, for example, who has threatened her self-esteem in some way and where at some level she engages in self-depreciation. By contrast, when the person makes herself unhealthily angry in the non-ego domain, she is angry at someone, for example, who has acted in some way that she finds offensive, but which does not pose a threat to her self-esteem and where she does not engage in self-depreciation. To complicate matters a little, it is possible for a person to make herself unhealthily angry in both ego and non-ego domains about the same event.

So, as I have stated, it is not what happens to the person or her inference about what happens to her that makes her unhealthily angry. Rather, the missing link is her irrational beliefs about the actual events or her inferences about these events.

Irrational beliefs in unhealthy ego anger

So what irrational beliefs does the person have to hold and rehearse in order to make herself experience unhealthy ego anger? The following three are the most relevant:

- a rigid demand (e.g. 'you must not criticise me')
- a self-depreciation belief (e.g. 'your criticism makes me stupid') and
- an other-depreciation belief (e.g. 'you are a bad person for criticising me *and for reminding me that I am stupid*').

Irrational beliefs in unhealthy non-ego anger

And how does a person make herself unhealthily angry in the non-ego domain? By holding and rehearsing the following irrational beliefs:

- a rigid demand (e.g. 'I must get to my meeting on time')
- a low frustration tolerance (LFT) belief (e.g. 'If I don't get to my meeting on time I couldn't bear it') and either
- an other-depreciation belief ('e.g. You are rotten for blocking me from getting to my meeting in time) if another person or other people are involved) or
- a life-conditions depreciation belief (e.g. 'Conditions are rotten for blocking me from getting to my meeting on time').

I will now take the above and show you how a person makes herself unhealthily angry about the inferences that I discussed earlier in the chapter. In doing so I will outline the general irrational belief involved and illustrate it with a specific example.

Unhealthy anger about other(s) transgressing socially agreed rules, legal rules and one's own personal rules

In general, when a person makes herself unhealthily angry about another person, for example, transgressing a socially agreed rule, a legal rule or one of her own rules, she needs to hold a rigid demand about such a transgression and an accompanying other-depreciation belief:

- The person must not jump the queue and he is a selfish rotten person for doing so (person breaks socially agreed rule).
- The person absolutely should not have driven through a red light and is an inconsiderate bastard for doing so (person breaks legal rule).
- The person absolutely should not have turned up late for an appointment with me and is a swine for doing so (person breaks her own personal rule).

The person will increase her unhealthy anger about these transgressions by holding the following additional irrational belief: 'Not only must you not break this rule in the first place, but you must not get away with it without being punished in the second place. If you do get away with it, then that is unfair and this must not be allowed to happen. I can't stand you and the world for allowing you to get away with it.' I will return to this theme of unfairness later in the chapter and show you how a person makes herself unhealthily angry about the injustices and unfairness of life.

Unhealthy anger about being blocked or frustrated in one's progress towards a goal

When a person makes herself unhealthily angry about being blocked or frustrated in her progress towards a goal, she holds a rigid demand and an LFT belief. In cases where she considers that another person is responsible for blocking her path towards her goal she can make herself unhealthily angry towards them by additionally holding an other-depreciation belief. Alternatively, in other cases where the person considers that she is responsible for the frustration, then she makes herself unhealthily angry at herself by additionally holding a self-depreciation belief.

Here are some examples:

- 'I must not be stuck in the traffic jam (rigid demand) and I can't stand it that I am (LFT belief). Whoever is responsible for this is a bastard (other-depreciation belief).'
- 'Fred blocked my promotions. He absolutely should not have done this (rigid demand) and he is a swine for doing so (other-depreciation belief).'

- 'I missed my train connection because I left home too late. I absolutely should not have done this (rigid demand) and I am an idiot for doing so (self-depreciation belief).'

Unhealthy anger about injustice or unfairness

In general, in order to make herself unhealthily angry about injustice or unfairness, a person once again needs to hold a rigid demand and an LFT belief about such a situation and a depreciation belief against the person, people or organisation she deems to be responsible for the injustice/unfairness. For example:

- 'I was promised a raise if I worked overtime. I worked overtime but was not given the promised raise. My boss absolutely should not be so unfair to me (rigid demand). It is intolerable (LFT belief) and he is a bastard for breaking his promise (other-depreciation belief).'
- 'I was prosecuted for a crime that I did not commit. The justice system stinks for doing something to me (depreciation belief about life conditions) that it absolutely should not have done (rigid demand).'
- 'A colleague of mine was prosecuted for a crime that she did not commit. The police are bastards (other-depreciation belief) for doing something to her that they absolutely should not have been allowed to get away with (rigid demand). I can't tolerate this injustice (LFT belief).'

Unhealthy anger about a threat to her self-esteem

When a person makes herself unhealthily angry about a threat to her self-esteem, she tends to hold three irrational beliefs: (a) a rigid demand about the person threatening her self-esteem; (b) an other-depreciation belief about this person and (c) a self-depreciation belief (usually well hidden) that renders her vulnerable to the threat in the first place. Let me give you an example.

Someone criticised Brenda who felt unhealthily angry about this criticism. She made herself unhealthily angry about this because:

- She depreciated herself about this criticism by holding the following irrational belief: 'I must not be criticised and if I am it proves that I am an inadequate person.'

- She quickly covered up her feelings of inadequacy by holding the person who criticised her responsible for her feelings and depreciated that person as in the following irrational belief: 'You must not criticise me and remind me that I am an inadequate person and you are no good for doing so.'

Unhealthy anger about being treated with disrespect

When the person makes herself unhealthily angry about being treated with disrespect and that issue is ego-based or non-ego-based, she does the following:

- She holds the irrational belief that the other person must treat her with respect and if he doesn't, this proves that she is not worthy of respect.
- She holds the irrational belief that the other person must not treat her with disrespect and that he is a bastard for reminding her that she is not worthy of respect when he disrespects her.

If the issue is non-ego-based, the person's major concern is that the other person has transgressed her rule for being treated with respect. Thus, in order to make herself unhealthily angry about this, she holds demands that other person must not treat her with disrespect and that he is a bastard for so doing.

Thinking that stems from unhealthy anger-based irrational beliefs

When a person holds an unhealthy anger-based irrational belief about any of the factors I discussed earlier in this chapter, this belief will influence how she subsequently thinks in the following ways.

Overestimating the extent to which the other person acted deliberately and with malice towards one

After the person has made herself unhealthily angry about the wrong that another person has done to her, for example, and she reflects on what that person has done, she is likely to conclude (a) that he acted deliberately in that way towards her (rather than accidentally or because he saw things differently from her) and (b) that his behaviour was motivated with malicious intent. It may well be that the person thought that way originally and that this was a central feature of what she was unhealthily angry about; however, her irrational belief would strengthen her conviction that the other person was deliberately out to get her. Also her irrational belief would lead her to dwell on this inference for quite a while and increase the likelihood that the person would believe that she must exact revenge on the other person, thus deepening her unhealthy anger – and that should keep her going for quite a long time in the unhealthy anger stakes!

Viewing oneself as definitely right and the other person as definitely wrong

Once the person has made herself unhealthily angry about different versions that she and someone else had about an event, her unhealthy anger-based irrational belief will strengthen her in the idea that she was in the right and that the other person was in the wrong. She will then tend to focus on this and hold the following irrational beliefs:

- 'The other person absolutely should not have been wrong in the first place.'

and as the person attempts to persuade him that she was right and that he was wrong:

- 'He must listen to reason and admit that he was wrong.'

Refusing to listen to or see the other person's point of view

When a person holds an unhealthy anger-based irrational belief about what someone else has done and is in dialogue with that person, she focuses on communicating why she is right and as such she will tend to refuse to listen to the other person's point of view. Even if she does listen to the other person, her unhealthy anger will interfere with her attempt to understand this viewpoint. He is wrong and thus his explanations are not worthy of consideration.

Developing and rehearsing revenge fantasies

Imagination is a powerful tool. Once a person is unhealthily angry, she will tend to use her imagination to develop and rehearse fantasies of exacting revenge. What the person does is the following:

1 She focuses on the situation where another person has wronged her.
2 She brings her unhealthy anger-creating irrational belief to this inference, for example: 'He absolutely should not have wronged me and he is a bastard for so doing.'
3 She shows herself that justice has to be achieved and that she has to get her revenge.
4 She thinks of ways of getting revenge and develops scenarios where she sees in her mind's eye her exacting revenge on the person who has wronged her.
5 She focuses on the sense of pleasure and power she gets when seeing herself, in her mind's eye, exacting revenge.

Every time the person rehearses a revenge fantasy, she strengthens her conviction in the following two anger-creating irrational beliefs:

- 'The other person is bad for doing what he absolutely should not have done to me.'
- 'When someone wrongs me, I must get my own back and punish that person.'

Behaviour that stems from unhealthy anger-based irrational beliefs

When a person holds unhealthy anger-based irrational beliefs, she will tend to act in certain ways. When she does act in these ways, she rehearses and therefore strengthens her conviction in these irrational beliefs.

Blaming the other person for making one unhealthily angry

When the person discusses her unhealthily angry feelings with friends and acquaintances, she tends to place the blame for her angry feelings on the behaviour of the person with whom she is unhealthily angry. She says things like 'He made me angry.' As it is unlikely that her friends will contradict her, this faulty notion remains unchecked and she will continue to refrain from taking responsibility for making herself unhealthily angry.

In dialogue with the other person whom she is unhealthily angry at, the person will also blame the other person for making her angry.

Attacking the other person verbally

After the person has made herself unhealthily angry about what another person has done to her, for example, she will feel an urge to attack her verbally. This can involve shouting and screaming at the person, making pejorative comments or just being generally unpleasant. When the person does some or all of these things, one of two things will happen. First, the other person may well make himself unhealthily angry about her verbal attack and attack her back. If this happens, then it is likely that the first person will make herself unhealthily angry about his verbal attack and will shout and scream back even more. Second, the other person may display signs that he feels hurt about her angry attacking behaviour. This then serves as a stimulus for the person to make herself feel guilty for hurting his feelings (see chapter 4).

Pursuing revenge

Revenge is sweet and pursuing it will certainly serve to strengthen the person's unhealthy anger-related irrational beliefs. When the person pursues revenge directly (by which I mean that the other person knows that she was the person who meted out revenge), she not only holds the belief that the other person absolutely should not have wronged her in the way that she did, she also holds one or more of the following irrational beliefs:

- 'The other person absolutely must not get away with his bad behaviour towards me.'
- 'The wrong towards me must be put right.'
- 'He must be punished for his behaviour towards me.'
- 'I must be the one to punish the other person and he must know that it was me who did it.'

Attacking the other person passive-aggressively

Gaining revenge can also be achieved indirectly. This is known as passive-aggressive behaviour and it also serves to reinforce the person's unhealthy anger-creating irrational beliefs. When a person is passive-aggressive in her attacks she gets revenge against the other person who realises that someone has attacked him, but doesn't know who. As such she is acting on the following irrational beliefs:

- 'The other person absolutely must not get away with his bad behaviour towards me.'
- 'The wrong towards me must be put right.'
- 'He must be punished for his behaviour towards me, but he must not know that I am the person who has attacked him.'

Recruiting allies against the other person

Another good way of paying someone back and strengthening the person's conviction in her unhealthy anger-creating irrational beliefs is to recruit allies against the other person. This may involve the person recruiting people to engage in a direct vengeful attack on the other, to deprive that person of their place in a social group or to besmirch the reputation of that person in the social community action. In all three cases the person will be acting on the irrational belief that the other person absolutely should not have wronged her or her reference group, is a bad person for so doing and thereby deserves to be paid back for their behaviour.

Expressing one's unhealthy anger cathartically

The counselling and psychotherapy field used to think that it was healthy for the person to express her unhealthy anger and that if she didn't, then she would turn her anger towards herself and make herself feel depressed. However, we now know that expressing unhealthy anger cathartically (i.e. with fully expressed feeling) only serves to make a person even angrier (in the unhealthy sense). This is because as she expresses her unhealthy anger she is rehearsing and thereby reinforcing her unhealthy anger-creating irrational beliefs. The answer to the question: 'How do you get to Carnegie Hall?' is 'Practise, practise, practise'. Similarly, the answer to the question: 'How do you make yourself unhealthily angry?' is 'Practise, practise, practise'. One way of practising is to express your anger cathartically.

Displacing one's unhealthy anger or 'kick the cat'

You have probably heard the phrase 'kicking the cat'. This refers to times when a person takes her unhealthy anger out on an innocent bystander. Doing so serves to reinforce her unhealthy anger-related irrational beliefs in a similar way to cathartic expression of unhealthy anger. When a person 'kicks the cat', she is expressing her unhealthy anger indirectly at the person with whom she has a problem. She does not express her unhealthily angry feelings directly at the person for a number of reasons, with anxiety heading the list.

Withdrawing aggressively

A final way in which the person acts when she is unhealthily angry, thus strengthening her unhealthy anger-creating irrational beliefs and thus making herself more prone to unhealthy anger, is to withdraw aggressively from situations in which she has made herself unhealthily angry. There are two major ways of withdrawing aggressively when a person is unhealthily angry. The first is for her to leave situations in which she feels unhealthy anger, demonstrating non-verbally that she is unhealthily angry. Brian, for example, used to make himself unhealthily angry in business meetings and stormed out of these meetings by banging the door as strongly as he could. Eventually he received verbal and written warnings about this before he sought help for his problem anger.

People develop and rehearse general unhealthy anger-based irrational beliefs

General unhealthy anger-based irrational beliefs are irrational beliefs that a person holds in many theme-related situations that result in her experiencing unhealthy anger in these situations. Developing and rehearsing such beliefs will lead the person to experience unhealthy anger in many different situations. She will do this mainly because she tends to make inferences, for example, that others have transgressed socially agreed, legal or her own personal rules, that others have frustrated her goal-directed efforts, that others have behaved unjustly or unfairly to her and/or to others and that others are posing a threat to her self-esteem.

Let me show you how this works. First, the person develops general unhealthy anger-based irrational beliefs such as: 'Other people must obey the rules and they are rotten people if they don't.' He then rehearses this general belief until he firmly believes it and brings it to relevant situations where it is possible that others may not obey the rules. Then, because he cannot convince himself that they will obey the rules, he tends to think that they have disobeyed the rules and they have done so intentionally and with malicious intent. Having created this unhealthy anger-based inference, the person then brings a specific version of this general unhealthy anger-based irrational belief to it and thereby makes himself feel unhealthy anger in the specific situation.

Let me give you a concrete example. Terence developed the following general unhealthy anger-based irrational belief: 'Others must respect me and if they don't, I am not worthy of respect and they are no good for showing this.' He took this belief to a specific situation where he was in a restaurant with a group of friends and a waiter asked everybody else for their order, but didn't ask Terence for his. His general unhealthy anger-based irrational belief led him to infer that the waiter showed him disrespect by not asking him for his order. It as if Terence reasoned: 'Because I can't convince myself that the waiter's failure to ask me for my order was an innocent error, then he showed me disrespect.' Terence's belief did not allow him to think that the waiter may have made a mistake.

Once Terence created his inference that he had been disrespected, he made himself unhealthily angry about it by holding a specific version of his general irrational belief. Thus 'The waiter showed me disrespect by not asking me for my order. He absolutely should have shown me respect and because he didn't, I am not a person worthy of respect and he is no good for demonstrating this.'

People develop and rehearse a view of the world founded on unhealthy anger-based irrational beliefs

You should now be familiar with the idea that people develop world views that render them vulnerable to particular unhealthy negative emotions. This is certainly the case with unhealthy anger. The world views that render a person vulnerable to unhealthy anger do so primarily because they make it very easy for her to make unhealthy anger-related inferences. Then, as I have shown you earlier in the chapter, the person makes herself unhealthily angry about these inferences with the appropriate irrational beliefs. Here is an illustrative list of the unhealthy anger-related world views that a person develops and the inferences that they spawn.

World view: It's a dog eat dog world.
Inference: People's actions will often be vicious and attacking.

World view: People only look after themselves and their own.
Inference: People's motives are primarily influenced by selfishness.

World view: There's no such thing as an accident. People always act with deliberation.
Inference: When people transgress the rules, they do so deliberately.

World view: People are out to get me, so I need to get them before they get me.
Inference: People's actions are designed to harm me.

Further reading

Academic

DiGiuseppe, R. & Tafrate, R.C. (2007). *Understanding anger disorders.* New York: Oxford University Press.

Self-help

Dryden, W. (1997). *Overcoming anger: When anger helps and when it hurts.* London: Sheldon.

In the next chapter, I will help you to understand hurt, an unhealthy emotion that often includes unhealthy anger.

Chapter 6

Understanding hurt

Hurt is an unhealthy negative emotion that a person is most likely to feel about the way that people significant to her behave (or fail to behave). I will follow the usual format in this chapter by first outlining the general steps that a person tends to take to make herself feel hurt before discussing each step in some detail.

How a person makes herself feel hurt: general steps

The steps a person takes to make herself feel hurt will now be familiar to you if you have read the foregoing chapters. Here they are as applied to hurt.

1   The person makes a hurt-related inference.
2   She brings a set of hurt-based irrational beliefs to that inference.
3   She thinks in ways that are consistent with the above irrational beliefs.
4   She acts in ways that are consistent with these irrational beliefs.
5   She rehearses a general version of her specific hurt-based irrational beliefs so that she is prone to make hurt-related inferences.
6   She develops and rehearses a hurt-based world view.

Now let me deal with these issues one at a time.

Hurt-related inferences

In order to feel hurt, a person needs to make one or more inferences about what is going on in her life. As I have repeatedly stressed, these inferences don't have to reflect accurately what happened. The important point is that the person believes that they are true.

What people tend to feel hurt about is what others (usually significant others) have done or have failed to do. What follows is a list of common hurt-related inferences about what people have done. It is important to note that the person feeling hurt considers that she does not deserve such behaviour at the hands of the other person. Indeed, it is very likely that the person considers that she deserves the very opposite.

Being unfairly criticised

While a person can feel hurt about unfair or fair criticism, she is more likely to feel hurt about a significant other criticising her unfairly. In addition, she is more likely to feel hurt about criticism that is directed to her as a person rather than criticism that is directed at her behaviour.

Being rejected

What a person finds particularly hurtful about being rejected is often the undeserved nature of the rejection. In doing so, the person tends to remind herself of all the good things that she has done for the other person and how she deserves far better. She tends to edit out all the things she may have done (or not done) that may have brought about her being rejected.

Sharon tended to ask her partner for things at very inconvenient times for him. She edited out the fact that her request was unreasonable and focused instead (a) on the fact that she was rejected and (b) on how she did not deserve to be rejected. Rather, she thought that she deserved to get her request met after all she had done for her partner in the past, to get what she asked for. For example, Sharon made sexual overtures to her partner at a time when he was exhausted and unlikely to respond sexually to her. In feeling hurt about being rejected, Sharon forgot about the untimeliness of her request and instead told herself that she had gone to a lot of trouble to make life pleasant for her partner and the least she deserved was some pleasure in return.

Being disapproved by the other person

Disapproval is similar to rejection in that they both involve another making some kind of negative judgement of the person, but they are different in that, in rejection, the other has cast the person aside, which he hasn't done yet when he disapproves of her. As with rejection, the person tends to feel more hurt when she thinks that the disapproval she receives is undeserved. Also, as with hurt, the person focuses on the undeserved nature of the disapproval rather than on what she may have done to provoke it.

Being betrayed by the other

Being betrayed by someone close to the person is a key hurt-related inference. Gina was a person who considered that she had been betrayed a lot in her life. On examination, this is what she tended to do. She placed absolute trust in people close to her and then told them all about her past, swearing them all not to tell a living soul. One or two people would violate this promise (but most wouldn't). Gina focused on the one or two that had 'betrayed' her and made herself feel hurt about this betrayal. What Gina did not appreciate was that if one takes a large number of people into one's confidence, statistically it is likely that one or two would break confidentiality. However, Gina focused on the betrayal rather than on the wisdom of indiscriminate secret-sharing.

The next list of hurt-related inferences concerns what other people fail to do. Once again, it is important to note that the person feeling hurt is likely to consider that she deserves far better treatment than what she is getting from the other person.

Being neglected

A person inferring that she has been neglected by someone close to her is a common hurt-related inference. People who consider that they have been neglected by others often play a part in this neglect. For example, Barbara used to take the lead with all of her friends in making social arrangements and continued to do this for a long period until her friends had grown used to the idea that she would do this in future. Then Barbara suddenly stopped making such arrangements without explaining why and waited for others to take over the reins of social secretary and to contact her about such arrangements. When they didn't (because they were waiting for her to take the lead as usual), she thought that she was being neglected by her friends and that, after all she had done for them, she didn't deserve such neglect. What Barbara failed to appreciate was her part in this 'neglect'.

Being unfairly excluded

Being unfairly excluded by a significant other when the person thinks she doesn't deserve to be is a common inference in hurt, particularly in three-person situations where all are friends, but two of the people have more in common than the third.

This happened to Felicity, who was friends with Gill and Tina and was the third person in this unbalanced triangle, in that Gill and Tina were closer with one another than they were with Felicity. In this situation, Felicity considered that she deserved to get equal attention from the two other people and that it was unfair for them to speak to each other for a lengthy period of time and exclude her.

Not being appreciated

Not being appreciated when she deserves to be is another common inference made by a person when she feels hurt. The person who makes this inference often disregards the reality of the situation where the person from whom appreciation is expected is not known for showing it. Heather did a lot for her boss, who was particularly unappreciative. When he didn't show her appreciation for what she did for him, Heather made herself feel hurt about the unfairness of his unappreciative behaviour.

Being deprived of what one wants when one thinks one has deserved it

As you have now seen, the concept of deservingness is an important one in situations about which a person makes herself feel hurt.

This concept can be applied to any situation where the person has been deprived of what she wants. If a person focuses on one of her relationships where she considers that she is not getting from them what she deserves, she will feel hurt about this deprivation as long as she brings her hurt-creating irrational beliefs (see below) to this undeserved deprivation.

The person holds and rehearses irrational beliefs about her hurt-related inference

You have probably grasped one of the main points of this book by now, which is that in order to make herself feel emotionally disturbed about something, it is necessary for a person to hold a disturbance-creating irrational belief about this something. The corollary of this is that situations or the inferences that the person makes about situations, while contributing to her disturbed feelings, do not on their own disturb her. Rather, the person disturbs herself about these situations (actual or inferred) by her irrational beliefs. Applying this to the topic of hurt, we can say that being unfairly excluded, for example, does not make a person feel hurt; rather, she makes herself feel hurt about unfair exclusion by the irrational beliefs that she holds about this actual or inferred event. Presently I will discuss what these irrational beliefs are.

Ego hurt and non-ego hurt

Before I do so, I want to make an important distinction between two types of hurt: ego hurt and non-ego hurt. When a person makes herself feel hurt in the ego domain she feels hurt because she is depreciating herself in some way for the undeserved treatment she has experienced at the hands of a significant other. By contrast, when a person makes herself feel hurt in the non-ego domain, she is focusing on how horrible the world is for allowing her to be treated in such an unfair way. She is not depreciating herself for this treatment; rather, she feels sorry for herself for the way she has been treated. To complicate matters, as with unhealthy anger, it is possible for a person to make herself feel hurt in both ego and non-ego domains about the same event.

Now let me discuss the irrational beliefs that lead to hurt in both these domains. Let me begin with ego hurt.

Irrational beliefs in ego hurt

To feel ego hurt a person needs at least two beliefs:

- a rigid demand (e.g. 'you must not reject me') and
- a self-depreciation belief (e.g. 'your rejection makes me unlovable').

Sometimes when unhealthy anger is a feature of hurt, the person also holds an other-depreciation belief (e.g. 'You are rotten for rejecting me since you are reminding me that I am unlovable').

Irrational beliefs in non-ego hurt

To feel non-ego hurt a person tends to hold:

- a rigid demand (e.g. 'You must not betray me')

and one, two or all of the following:

- an awfulising belief (e.g. 'It is awful that you betrayed me. Poor me, I don't deserve to be treated like this')
- a low frustration tolerance (LFT) belief (e.g. 'I can't stand being betrayed. Poor me, I don't deserve to be treated like this')
- a world-depreciation belief (e.g. 'The world is a rotten place for allowing such bad treatment to poor, undeserving me')
- an other-depreciation belief (e.g. 'You are a bad person for betraying me'). This is particularly the case where unhealthy anger is a feature of non-ego hurt.

Thinking that stems from hurt-based irrational beliefs

As I have discussed with the other unhealthy negative emotions, when a person holds a hurt-creating irrational belief about any of the factors I discussed earlier in this chapter, this belief will influence the way that she subsequently thinks in the following ways.

Overestimating the unfairness of the other person's behaviour

As I discussed earlier in this chapter, a person is much more likely to make herself feel hurt about being treated badly by those close to her when she considers that she does not deserve such treatment than when she thinks that she does. When she holds hurt-based irrational beliefs and when she thinks again about the way she has been treated by the other person, her tendency is to overestimate the unfairness in the way she has been treated. Specifically, she may think about all the good things she has done for the other person and edit out all the good things that they have done for her. Consequently, she will dwell on the unfair imbalance that her irrational beliefs lead her to focus on.

Remember that this bias is a feature of the original inference about which the person made herself feel hurt, but it is more pronounced after being processed, as it were, by the person's hurt-based irrational beliefs.

Seeing the other person as showing lack of care or showing indifference

When a person holds hurt-based irrational beliefs about the unfair treatment that she has experienced at the hands of someone close to her, she will tend to conclude that the reason why he treated her so badly is because he doesn't care about her or is indifferent towards her. She will then tend to focus on that lack of caring or indifference and may well disturb herself about this attitude by thinking irrationally about it.

Seeing oneself as alone, uncared for or misunderstood

When a person holds hurt-based irrational beliefs about being mistreated by a significant other, she will tend to see herself placed in a negative situation in relation to the world. This view is usually an overgeneralisation. When a person is mistreated and makes herself feel hurt about it, she will tend to see herself as alone in the world, uncared for in the world or misunderstood by the world. This negative situation will be coloured by ego-based hurt (e.g. 'I am uncared for in the world. This proves that I am not worth caring about') or by non-ego-based hurt (e.g. 'I am alone in the world. Poor me!').

Thinking of past 'hurts'

When a person has made herself feel hurt by holding a relevant hurt-based irrational belief, she tends to focus on past hurts. These 'hurts' may involve the other person who she currently feels hurt about or it may be broader and involve past 'hurts' with others in general. These 'hurts' may be similar in content to the specific incident the person currently feels hurt about (e.g. lack of appreciation) or it may be much broader and involve being mistreated, unappreciated, unfairly deprived, unfairly rejected by people.

Thinking that the other person has to put things right of their own accord

When I discuss sulking in the following section, I will point out that one of the purposes of such behaviour is to encourage the other person to take action of their own accord to put things right between him and the person who feels hurt and is sulking. Hurt-based irrational beliefs encourage the person to think this way. Here the person reminds herself that since she was unfairly treated (for example) by the other person, the fair thing for that person to do would be to make the first move. Thinking this way will also help to strengthen the person's conviction in her hurt-based irrational belief.

Behaviour that stems from hurt-based irrational beliefs

When a person holds hurt-based irrational beliefs, she will tend to act in certain ways. When she does act in these ways, she rehearses and therefore strengthens her conviction in these irrational beliefs.

Blaming the other person for making her feel hurt

As with unhealthy anger, when discussing her feelings of hurt with friends and acquaintances, the person tends to place the blame for her hurt feelings on the behaviour of the person with whom she feels hurt. She does not take responsibility for her own feelings in this respect. This prevents the person from taking steps to deal with her hurt feelings by identifying and changing her hurt-based irrational beliefs.

Shutting down direct channels of communication with the other person while communicating indirectly that the other person has 'hurt' her

When the person holds hurt-based irrational beliefs, then she tends to shut down direct channels of communication with the person with whom she feels hurt. The main point here is that the person does not tell the other what she feels hurt about, rather, she tends to *indirectly* show the other person how she feels. This is commonly known as sulking.

Sulking comes in two major forms. The first involves the person not talking to the other person at all. She can either do this loudly (e.g. by banging doors) or quietly (by silently rebuffing all attempts by the other person to engage her in direct communication). The second form of sulking involves the person criticising the other person but not telling that person what she feels hurt about.

As I showed in my book entitled *The Incredible Sulk* (Sheldon Press, 1992), sulking has a number of purposes that serve to maintain the person's hurt-based irrational beliefs if acted on.

- To punish the other for 'hurting' her feelings.
- To get what she wants from the other person.
- To get the other person to make the first move. (Part of the philosophy that underpins hurt is that the person has been treated unfairly by the other, whose responsibility it is to make efforts to find out how he has 'hurt' her and then to put things right between them. It is also part of this philosophy not to make this process too easy for the other person).
- To extract proof of caring from the other person. (Here the other has to prove that they care about the person by making continued attempts to get her to talk. If he doesn't do this or gives up too easily, the person has something else to make herself feel hurt about).
- To protect herself from further hurt. (By doing this the person is practising her hurt-creating irrational belief indirectly – it is as if she is saying: 'I need to stop communicating with this other person because if I continue to communicate with him,

he will keep acting in ways that I will feel hurt about. Thus, I'll stop communicating').

- To restore a sense of power. (Here sulking is an attempt by the person to get the upper hand in the relationship with the other who in her mind has 'hurt' her. In doing so, she reinforces her hurt-creating irrational beliefs).

People develop and rehearse general hurt-based irrational beliefs

General hurt-based irrational beliefs are irrational beliefs that a person holds in many theme-related situations that result in her experiencing hurt in these situations. Developing and rehearsing such beliefs will lead the person to experience hurt in a variety of different situations. She will do this mainly because she tends to make inferences, for example, that those close to her do not appreciate her or have treated her unfairly.

Let me show you how this works. First, the person develops a general hurt-based irrational belief (in this case in the non-ego domain) such as: 'Those close to me must include me in everything that they do and it's terrible if they don't. Poor me if I am excluded.' She then rehearses this general belief until she firmly believes it and brings it to relevant situations where it is possible that others may not include her. Then, because she cannot convince herself that they will include her or that there is a good reason for her exclusion, she will tend to think that they have unfairly excluded her and have done so intentionally. Having created this hurt-based inference, the person then brings a specific version of this general hurt-based irrational belief to it and thereby makes herself feel hurt in the specific situation.

Let me give you a concrete example. Fay developed the following general hurt-based irrational belief: 'Because I would not betray the trust of those close to me, they must not betray my trust and if they do, the world is a rotten place for allowing this to happen to poor, undeserving me.' She took this belief to a specific situation where she learned that her sister, whose confidences she had kept in the past, *may* have told a group of their mutual friends, when drunk, something that Fay told her in strict confidence. Fay's general hurt-based irrational belief led her to infer that her sister did, in fact, betray her trust. It as if Fay reasoned: 'Because I can't convince myself that my sister did not betray my trust, then she did. If she did so, she betrayed my trust intentionally.' Fay's irrational belief did not allow her to think that her sister did not betray her trust or that if she did, she did so unintentionally because she was drunk. Once Fay created this inference that she had been betrayed, she made herself feel hurt about it by holding a specific version of her general irrational belief. Thus: 'My sister betrayed my trust intentionally by telling our mutual friends something that I told her in confidence. She absolutely should not have betrayed me and the world is a rotten place for allowing this to happen to poor, undeserving me.'

People develop and rehearse a view of the world founded on hurt-based irrational beliefs

The world views that render a person vulnerable to feelings of hurt do so, as I have pointed out throughout this book, primarily because they make it very easy for the person to make hurt-related inferences. Then the person makes herself feel hurt about these inferences with the appropriate irrational beliefs. Here is an illustrative list of the hurt-related world views that a person develops and the inferences that they spawn.

World view: When I do a lot for those close to me, they will fail to reciprocate.
Inference: People close to me will let me down.

World view: If I trust those close to me they will often betray me, while I would not betray them.
Inference: People close to me will betray me.

World view: Significant others will act unfairly towards me, while I would not be unfair to them.
Inference: I will not get what I deserve from significant others.

World view: Those close to me will often exclude or neglect me for no good reason.
Inference: If I learn that people close to me are doing things with each other when I have not been invited, this is evidence that I have been excluded or neglected.

Further reading

Academic

Vangelisti, A. (Ed.) (In press). *Feeling hurt in close relationships.* New York: Cambridge University Press.

Self-help

Dryden, W. (2007). *Overcoming hurt.* London: Sheldon.

In the next chapter, I will discuss unhealthy jealousy.

Chapter 7

Understanding unhealthy jealousy

Unhealthy jealousy ruins relationships! If a person has a problem with unhealthy jealousy, she will make it very difficult for anyone to have an ongoing love relationship with her. In fact, in order for someone to sustain an ongoing relationship with the person, they will have to have the patience of a saint and either low self-esteem or an unhealthy need to help the person overcome her jealousy problem.

Before I discuss the nature of unhealthy jealousy, let me again discuss terminology. As with anger, we don't have very good words to discriminate between unhealthy and healthy jealousy, so I will use these two terms here.

By *unhealthy jealousy*, I mean a state where a person demands that her partner must only have eyes for her and must not show interest in anyone who she deems to be a love rival. The person's inclination is to monitor her partner closely for signs that he is interested in another person, question him closely to this effect and either check on his whereabouts or restrict his movements.

By contrast, *healthy jealousy* is a state where the person prefers that her partner only has eyes for her and not show interest in anyone who she deems to be a love rival, but does not insist that this must be the case. Her inclination is to assume that her partner is not interested in another person unless she has clear evidence to the contrary and if she does, she will confront her partner with her evidence in a clear, assertive way. In general, she will neither monitor her partner closely for signs that he is interested in another person, question him closely to this effect nor check on his whereabouts or restrict his movements.

How a person makes herself unhealthily jealous: general steps

The steps that a person needs to take to make herself unhealthily jealous will be very familiar to you by now, since they are the same as I outlined in the previous chapters. As an overview, here they are applied to unhealthy jealousy.

1   The person makes an unhealthy jealousy-related inference.
2   She brings a set of unhealthy jealousy-based irrational beliefs to that inference.
3   She thinks in ways that are consistent with the above irrational beliefs.
4   She acts in ways that are consistent with these irrational beliefs.
5   She rehearses a general version of her specific unhealthy jealousy-based irrational beliefs so that she is prone to make unhealthy jealousy-based inferences with respect to her relationship(s).
6   She develops and rehearses an unhealthy jealousy-based world view.

I will now deal with these issues one at a time. As I do, I will concentrate on unhealthy romantic jealousy.

Unhealthy jealousy-related inferences

To feel unhealthily jealous, a person needs first to focus on a scenario (which can be real or imagined) that has three people in it: the person, her partner (a term that I use broadly here) and another person who she sees as an actual or potential love rival. Then the person makes an inference that the other person poses a threat to her relationship with her partner. The nature of this threat is likely to be fivefold.

'My partner will leave me'

The person regards the other person in the triangle as someone who will replace her in the affections of her partner and thinks that her partner will leave her for the other person.

'I'm not the most important person in his life'

The person thinks that her partner finds the other person more attractive than her and that she will be displaced as the most important person in her partner's life (even though she does not think that he will go off with the other person).

'I'm not his one and only'

The person acknowledges that it is important to her that her partner is only interested in her and that his interest in the other person means that she is no longer his one and only.

'Someone is showing an interest in him/her'

The person acknowledges that it is important to her that no one (who has the potential to be a love rival) shows an interest in her partner, so when someone does she deems this to be a threat.

'I don't know what he/she is doing or thinking'

Here the person realises that unless she places her partner under constant surveillance (which she may well like to do!), she will not know what he is doing. Indeed, even if she does manage to know at all times what her partner is doing, it is unlikely that she will ever know for sure what he is thinking. Thus, uncertainty about her partner is a key inference in unhealthy jealousy.

As I have mentioned several times, these inferences don't have to reflect accurately what is happening or what happened. In fact, when a person is feeling unhealthily jealous, her inferences are likely to be false. This doesn't matter too much, for the important point is that she has to think that they are true.

The person holds and rehearses irrational beliefs about her unhealthy jealousy-related inference

You will now not need reminding that a person's unhealthy jealousy is not caused by her inference that her partner may find another woman attractive, for example. Rather, these unhealthy feelings are largely determined by the irrational beliefs that the person holds about this inference, true or not.

Let me discuss these points with reference to Sylvia, who was uncertain about what her partner was doing at his office party, to which she had not been invited. She brought the following irrational beliefs to this uncertainty, which were in the area of non-ego disturbance (where the person's problem was not related to her view of herself).

- a rigid demand (e.g. 'I must know that my partner does not find anyone at the party attractive')
- an LFT (e.g. 'I can't stand not knowing that my partner does not find anyone at the party attractive').

As I will discuss later in this chapter, these unhealthy jealousy-based irrational beliefs led Sylvia to conclude that under these circumstances her partner did find other women at the party attractive and that, for example, this meant that she was not the one and only person that he finds attractive. Then she focused on this situation and held the following irrational beliefs (which were in the area of ego disturbance, where she depreciated herself in some way):

- a rigid demand (e.g. 'My partner must find only me attractive')
- a self-depreciation belief (e.g. 'If my partner finds other women attractive, this means that I am unattractive and worthless').

Here are similar irrational beliefs about the other inferences I discussed earlier. Thus:

- 'My partner must not leave me. If s/he does, it proves that I am unlovable.'
- 'I must be the most important person in my partner's life. If I'm not, then I am nothing.'
- 'I must be my partner's one and only. If I am not, then I am worthless.'

The above irrational beliefs exemplify ego disturbance.

When a person holds an irrational belief about other people showing an interest in her partner, this is more frequently in the area of non-ego disturbance. Thus:

- 'Nobody else must show an interest in my partner. If they do, it's terrible'.
- 'Nobody else must show an interest in my partner. If they do, they are no good.'

Thinking that stems from unhealthy jealousy-based irrational beliefs

When a person holds an unhealthy jealousy-creating irrational belief about any of the factors I discussed earlier in this chapter, this belief will influence the ways in which she subsequently thinks about relevant aspects of the total situation.

Here are some common examples of such subsequent thinking.

Distrusting and being suspicious of one's partner

When a person is feeling unhealthily jealous, she tends to think that whatever her partner says or does, he is not to be trusted. In this frame of mind, she looks for discrepancies in what her partner says and/or does. This will be particularly the case when she keeps note of his or her movements, which provides her with what she considers to be the necessary ammunition. When she finds a discrepancy, however small, she tends to remind herself that this is evidence that her partner cannot be trusted.

Thinking of relevant people as love rivals

When a person has made herself unhealthily jealous about her partner in one context, she can unwittingly maintain her unhealthy jealousy problem by thinking that relevant people (e.g. all attractive women) are potential love rivals. Doing this results in the person seeing that her relationship with her partner is always under threat – one of the main features of a chronic unhealthy jealousy problem.

Thinking that one's partner has a negative attitude towards one

The person's unhealthy jealousy-related irrational beliefs will lead her to think that her partner has a negative attitude towards her. She will then tend to think of all the negative things that he has said about her. This will reinforce the irrational belief that she is not worth caring about.

Thinking in distorted ways about one's partner's behaviour

Once a person has made herself unhealthily jealous about her partner's behaviour (for example, about him talking to an attractive woman at a social gathering), she tends to think in negatively distorted ways about her partner's behaviour, which serves to maintain her unhealthy jealous feelings. Thus, in the above example, the person will tend to think one or more of the following:

- He wants to have an affair with her.
- He is betraying me.
- He is rejecting me.
- He is making me look a fool in the eyes of other people.

Thinking in such distorted ways will increase the chances that the person will perpetuate her unhealthy jealous feelings, particularly if she holds irrational beliefs about these distortions (e.g. 'By talking to that woman, which he must not do, my partner is rejecting me and this proves that I am worthless').

Thinking in distorted ways about one's future relationships

Once a person has made herself unhealthily jealous about her present relationship, she also tends to think in negatively distorted ways about potential future relationships. Thus, when the person feels unhealthily jealous about her partner's unfaithful behaviour (real or more likely imagined), for example, she thinks that any future partners she might have will also act in the same ways and that she will never have a relationship with someone who will be faithful to her.

Thinking negatively about one's own qualities (particularly in relation to possible love rivals)

When the person has made herself unhealthily jealous she tends to think negatively about her own qualities. Thus, when Linda felt unhealthily jealous about her partner talking to an attractive woman, she thought that, by comparison, she is unattractive, uninteresting and unintelligent. These negative thoughts will tend to fuel her self-depreciation beliefs and thus increase the chances that she will make herself unhealthily jealous in the future.

Thinking positively about the qualities of one's love rivals (particularly in relation to oneself)

A companion to thinking negatively about herself when the person is unhealthily jealous is thinking positively about the qualities of potential love rivals. Thus, when Sylvia felt unhealthily jealous about her partner talking to an attractive woman, she thought that, by comparison, the other woman was attractive, interesting and intelligent. These thoughts will again help fuel her self-depreciation beliefs and thus increase the chances that she will make herself unhealthily jealous in the future.

Like a lot of people with a jealousy problem, Sylvia combined thinking negatively about herself with thinking positively about her love rival. In doing so, she doubled the chances that she would make herself unhealthily jealous in the future.

Behaviour that stems from unhealthy jealousy-based irrational beliefs

When a person holds unhealthy jealousy-based irrational beliefs, she will tend to act in certain ways. When she does act in these ways, she rehearses and therefore strengthens her conviction in these irrational beliefs.

Questioning her partner constantly, but not accepting what he says

The person's unhealthy jealousy-based irrational beliefs will lead her to question her partner about his feelings, thoughts and behaviours, particularly with respect to any potential love rivals. When he answers her questions, the person tends not to believe the veracity of his responses. She will look for any inconsistencies in what her partner says and ask further questions about these inconsistencies.

If her partner refuses to answer her questions, she may well accuse him of being unfaithful to her. When he denies these accusations, she will take what he says and ask further questions. She may well keep this process going until her partner storms off.

When she next sees him, she may also tell him that his storming off is proof that he had been unfaithful to her.

Checking on one's partner constantly

When the person is not in her partner's presence, her unhealthy jealousy-related irrational beliefs will lead her to make checks on him. There are a number of ways in which she can do this. Thus, she can:

- Follow her partner surreptitiously.
- Telephone her partner. Mobile phones are particularly useful in this respect.
- Get reports on her partner's activities from friends. If she is wealthy, she may hire a private investigator.

Her checking behaviours will have the effect of maintaining her unhealthy jealousy by keeping in her mind that there is a threat to her relationship with her partner and, if she doesn't know what her partner is doing, for example, that he is up to no good. Having constructed these thoughts, the person may well hold irrational beliefs about them, thus entrenching her unhealthy jealousy.

Monitoring one's partner closely when in his presence

When a person is with her partner, her unhealthy jealousy-based irrational beliefs will lead her to monitor her partner closely, particularly when in the presence of potential love rivals. These irrational beliefs will also encourage her to assume that her partner is looking at one such rival if she sees him glancing in the rival's general direction and to further assume that her partner is interested in the rival. Such monitoring will keep the idea in the person's mind that threats to her relationship with her partner are everywhere, a key component of unhealthy jealousy.

The person may also tend to monitor the behaviour and gaze direction of her potential love rivals and assume that they are interested in her partner even in the absence of corroborating evidence.

Accusing one's partner of indiscretions and infidelities

A person's unhealthy jealousy-related irrational beliefs will also encourage her to accuse her partner of various indiscretions and infidelities. If she does this frequently, her partner will eventually withdraw from her because he finds her behaviour aversive. The person will then take his withdrawal as evidence that he is interested in someone else. The person will then accuse him of this, and doing so will again increase her conviction that threats to her relationship are ubiquitous. She will, in all probability, bring her irrational beliefs to this conclusion to deepen her unhealthy jealousy.

Setting traps for one's partner

One of my clients who had a problem with unhealthy jealousy suspected that her husband was interested in other women. So she introduced him to an attractive woman at a works party, whom she knew delighted in sleeping with other women's husbands. She then left the party, claiming to have a migraine, but insisted that her husband stay and give the woman a lift home. When he came home, she accused him of sleeping with the woman, even though he neither had the time nor the interest in doing so. In short, my client's unhealthy jealousy-based irrational beliefs led her to set a trap for her husband. This only served to reinforce my client's irrational beliefs. It is clear, then, that setting traps for her partner will serve to perpetuate her unhealthy jealousy, and have a very negative impact on her relationship. If she sets such traps for her partner frequently, he may leave her. While she will conclude that she was right all along that he was interested in other women, the reality is that her behaviour served to make her relationship unsustainable from her partner's point of view. Sadly, when in the grips of unhealthy jealousy, the person is so blinkered that she cannot see what is obvious to others.

Placing restrictions on one's partner

When a person holds unhealthy jealousy-based irrational beliefs, doing so will lead her to place restrictions on her partner that effectively stop him engaging in activities that *she* finds threatening.

For example, Laragh feared that her partner would talk to and show interest in potential love rivals at social gatherings to which she had not been invited and thus banned her partner from attending these functions. In doing so, she reinforced her unhealthy jealousy because by placing restrictions on her partner she was acting on the following ideas: 'I forbid you to attend social gatherings without me because:

- If you go, I will not know what you are getting up to and I need to know that you are not showing interest in a potential love rival because if I don't know this I will assume that you are showing a romantic interest in this person and
- If you do talk to someone that I deem to be a love rival, this means that you prefer them to me and I couldn't stand that.'

Retaliating

Another way that the person acts on and thereby reinforces her unhealthy jealousy and the irrational beliefs that underpin it is by retaliating against her partner's presumed infidelities. I say 'presumed' here because the person may have very little actual evidence that her partner has been unfaithful to her. This doesn't really matter since what does matter is that she thinks that he has been unfaithful. Given this, her irrational beliefs lead her to be unfaithful herself as a way of getting back at her partner. She might even get her retaliation in first and have an affair before she discovers that her partner has been unfaithful to her, after all, she concludes, it is only a matter of time before s/he does.

Retaliating against her partner (before or after the event) serves to keep to the forefront of the person's mind the notion that there is an ever-present threat to her relationship to which she will easily bring her irrational beliefs to create and perpetuate ever-present unhealthy jealousy.

Punishing one's partner

Retaliation helps to perpetuate unhealthy jealousy in that inherent in the idea of retaliating against her partner is the inference that he has been unfaithful to the person (or will inevitably be so in the future). When she punishes her partner she also assumes that he has been unfaithful to her in some way, thus strengthening the idea in her mind that threats to her relationship are ubiquitous, a conclusion to which she brings her irrational beliefs. Such punishments are particularly potent when the person does not disclose why she is punishing her partner. Here, you will notice some overlap between unhealthy jealousy and feelings of hurt (see chapter 6), particularly when the person punishes her partner by refusing to communicate with him (i.e. punishment by sulking). Another way of punishing her partner for being unfaithful to her is to verbally berate him and is common when the person also clings to the notion that anything that he may say in his defence is a lie!

Punishing one's love rival

Punishing her rival for taking her partner away from her (for this is how the person inaccurately sees it in her mind) is another behaviour that stems from the person's unhealthy jealousy-based irrational beliefs and serves to keep her unhealthy jealousy alive. It is important to recognise that when the person's problem jealousy is chronic, such punishment frequently happens when there is no evidence at all that the rival has taken the partner from her. The 'evidence' is all in the person's imagination. Exacting such punishment also serves to keep in her mind the notion that rivals to her partner's affections are omnipresent and are likely to be successful and thus gives the person a further opportunity to rehearse her unhealthy jealousy-related irrational beliefs, which she easily brings to such inferences.

People develop and rehearse general unhealthy jealousy-based irrational beliefs

General unhealthy jealousy-based irrational beliefs are irrational beliefs that a person holds in many theme-related situations that enable her to experience unhealthy jealousy in these situations. Developing and rehearsing such beliefs will enable the person to experience unhealthy jealousy in many different situations. She will do this mainly because she makes frequent inferences that she is facing a threat to her relationship with her partner in the absence of corroborative evidence.

Let me show you how this works. First, the person needs to develop a general unhealthy jealousy-based irrational belief such as: 'My partner must only show interest in me and if he shows interest in someone else it means that I am unworthy.' She then rehearses this general belief until she firmly believes it and brings it to relevant situations where it is possible that her partner may show interest in someone else. Then, because she cannot convince herself that her partner is not interested in the other person, she will tend to think that he is and furthermore that the other person is interested in her partner and that they want to begin a relationship with one another. Having created this unhealthy jealousy-based inference, the person then brings a specific version of this general unhealthy jealousy-based irrational belief to it and thereby makes herself feel unhealthy jealousy in the specific situation.

Let me give you a concrete example of how to do this. Samantha developed the following general unhealthy jealousy-based irrational belief: 'I must know at all times what my partner is doing and it's terrible if I don't know this.' She took this belief to a specific situation where her partner left a message on her answerphone saying that he would be home late from work. Her general unhealthy jealousy-based irrational belief led her to infer that her partner was out with a potential love rival. It is as if Samantha reasoned: 'Because I don't know what my partner is doing and it is terrible not to know, not knowing means that he is with someone else.' Her rigid irrational belief did not readily allow her to think that her partner was doing something completely innocent like working late on his own. Once Samantha created her inference that her partner was with a love rival, it was fairly easy for her to make herself feel unhealthily jealous bringing the following specific unhealthy jealousy-based irrational belief to it. Thus: 'My partner is with someone else tonight. He must not do this and because he is, it proves that I am worthless.'

Samantha then acted according to this irrational belief and when he came home accused her partner of meeting a woman and verbally berated him when he denied this.

People develop and rehearse a view of the world founded on unhealthy jealousy-based irrational beliefs

The world views that render a person vulnerable to unhealthy jealousy do so again because they make it very easy for her to make unhealthy jealousy-related inferences. Then, as I have shown you earlier in the chapter, she makes herself unhealthily jealous about these inferences with the appropriate irrational beliefs. Here is an illustrative list of unhealthy jealousy-related world views and the inferences that they spawn.

World view: Partners will ultimately leave.
Inference: My partner is on the look out for someone better.

World view: Partners are basically untrustworthy.
Inference: Whatever my partner says about his feelings towards me and love rivals is not to be taken at face value.

World view: If I trust someone they will make a fool of me. So I need to always be on my guard.
Inference: When my partner asks me to trust him, he is up to no good.

World view: Not knowing what partners are feeling, thinking and doing is very dangerous.
Inference: If I don't know what my partner is feeling, thinking or doing in, this means that he is interested in someone else and/or thinking of leaving me.

Further reading

Academic

Salovey, P. (Ed.). (1991). *The psychology of jealousy and envy.* New York: Guilford.

Self-help

Dryden, W. (1998). *Overcoming jealousy.* London: Sheldon.

In the next chapter, I will discuss unhealthy envy. Unhealthy envy and unhealthy jealousy are often used interchangeably, but as you will see they are different emotions.

Chapter 8

Understanding unhealthy envy

Unhealthy envy is a particularly destructive emotion. It can sour relationships and lead a person to become obsessed with what she doesn't have in life, leaving her to take for granted or neglect what she does have in life. As we will see, it can also lead a person to destroy or spoil what others have.

Before I discuss the nature of unhealthy envy, I need to once again discuss terminology. As with anger and jealousy, we don't have very good words to discriminate between unhealthy and healthy envy, so I will use these two terms here.

By *unhealthy envy*, I mean a state where a person demands that she must have what she covets in others' lives. Her inclination is to aim to get what she lacks at all costs or, if not, to spoil or destroy things for others.

By contrast, *healthy envy* is a state where the person would like to have what she covets in others' lives, but does not demand that she must get it. Her inclination is to strive for what she wants as long as it is healthy to do so and she experiences no desire to spoil or destroy things for others.

How a person makes herself unhealthily envious: general steps

The steps that a person needs to take to make herself unhealthily envious will be well known to you by now, but I will review them for the last time as they apply to unhealthy envy.

1   The person makes an unhealthy envy-related inference.
2   She brings a set of unhealthy envy-based irrational beliefs to that inference.

3   She thinks in ways that are consistent with the above irrational beliefs.
4   She acts in ways that are consistent with these irrational beliefs.
5   She rehearses a general version of her specific unhealthy envy-based irrational beliefs so that she easily tends to make unhealthy envy-based inferences about what others have.
6   She develops and rehearses an unhealthy envy-based world view.

I will now deal with these issues one at a time.

Unhealthy envy-related inferences

To feel unhealthily envious, the person needs to focus on a scenario (which can be real or imagined) that has three elements to it, usually: the person herself, another person (or people) and something or someone that the other has that the person prizes but does not have. Envy is often confused with jealousy, which, as I showed in the previous chapter, involves the person thinking that she faces a threat to her relationship with her partner. I often explain the difference in the following way. I am bald and I would like to have a full head of hair. Now, imagine that I meet a man with a full head of hair. If I were envious of the person's hair, I would be saying that I would like a full head of hair like the other person. If I were jealous of the person's hair I would be saying that I think that the person's hair (not the person himself) poses a threat to my relationship with my partner – clearly a ridiculous notion.

Here are a number of envy scenarios to show the range of things a person can be envious of.

- Barry was envious of his friend's attractive wife (object of envy: a person).
- Linda was envious of her friend's good looks (object of envy: physical characteristics).
- Muriel was envious of her married friends' family life (object of envy: family life).
- Phil was envious of his friend's promotion (object of envy: achievement).

- Mr and Mrs Smith were envious of their friend's lavish lifestyle (object of envy: lifestyle).
- Ben was envious of his friend's extraversion (object of envy: personal characteristic).
- Jane was envious of Beryl's ability to play the piano (object of envy: talent).
- Bill was envious of his friend's Porsche (object of envy: possession).

As I have mentioned several times before in this book, these inferences do not have to reflect reality. This doesn't matter too much, for the important point is that the person has to think that they are true.

The person holds and rehearses irrational beliefs about her unhealthy envy-related inference

Once again I want to stress that a person's unhealthy envy is not caused by her inference that another person has something that she wants but does not have. Rather, these unhealthy feelings are largely determined by the irrational beliefs that the person holds about this inference, true or not. So let me show you how to feel unhealthily envious by detailing which irrational beliefs to develop and rehearse about the above inferences.

There are, in fact, two different types of unhealthy envy: ego envy and non-ego envy, although a person may have both.

Unhealthy ego envy

In ego envy the person tends to invest her self-esteem in whatever it is that others have that she wants, but doesn't have. In order to make herself unhealthily envious in the ego domain, she needs to hold two irrational beliefs:

- a rigid demand (e.g. 'A colleague got promoted and I absolutely should get promoted as well')
- a self-depreciation belief (e.g. 'I am less worthy than my colleague for not getting promoted').

Unhealthy non-ego envy

In non-ego envy, the person disturbs herself about not having what she wants. She does not invest her self-esteem in whatever she doesn't have. In order to make herself unhealthily envious in the non-ego domain, she needs to hold two irrational beliefs:

- a rigid demand (e.g. 'A colleague got promoted and I absolutely should get promoted as well')
- low frustration tolerance (LFT) (e.g. 'I can't stand the situation where my colleague got promoted and I didn't').

The importance of focus in unhealthy envy and the impact on irrational beliefs

So far I have concentrated on discussing unhealthy envy, when the focus is on the person wanting what someone else has and she does not have and then bringing a set of irrational beliefs to this situation. The person can also change the focus so that it is on her wanting the other person not to have what she doesn't have, and then making herself unhealthily envious about this state of affairs. Let's take the example I have just discussed, where a work colleague has just been promoted and the person hasn't. I have shown how the person can make herself unhealthily envious by believing: 'I must get promoted like my colleague', but she can also make herself unhealthily envious by changing the focus of the situation so that she believes: 'My colleague absolutely should not have been promoted when I wasn't.'

The role of irrational beliefs in unhealthy envy: the examples revisited

Let me now illustrate the above by returning to the examples I outlined earlier. I will assume that in all the scenarios the envy experienced was unhealthy in nature.

- Barry was unhealthily envious of his friend's attractive wife (object of envy: a person).
  Barry's unhealthy envy was largely non-ego in nature. He thus held the following irrational beliefs: 'I must have an attractive wife like my friend has and I can't stand not having one.'

- Linda was unhealthily envious of her friend's good looks (object of envy: physical characteristics).

  Linda's unhealthy envy was largely ego in nature. She held the following irrational beliefs: 'I must be as attractive as my friend and I am less worthy than her because I am not.'

  [This example shows the comparative aspect of envy as Linda is judging herself to be less worthy than her friend because she considers herself to be less attractive than the other.]

- Muriel was envious of her married friends' family life (object of envy: family life).

  Muriel's unhealthy envy was both ego and non-ego in nature. She believed the following: 'I must have a family like my friends do. Not having what I want in this regard is intolerable (non-ego) and proves that I am unlovable (ego).'

- Phil was envious of his friend's promotion (object of envy: achievement).

  Phil's unhealthy envy was largely ego in nature. He held the following irrational beliefs: 'My friend absolutely should not have been promoted when I didn't. The fact that he did and I didn't proves that I am a rotten person.'

- Mr and Mrs Smith were envious of their friend's lavish lifestyle (object of envy: lifestyle).

  Mr and Mrs Smith's unhealthy envy was largely non-ego in nature and was based on the following shared irrational beliefs: 'Our friends must not have the lifestyle that we don't have and we can't stand it that they do and we don't.'

- Ben was envious of his friend's extraversion (object of envy: personal characteristic).

  Ben's unhealthy envy was largely ego in nature. He believed the following: 'I must be more outgoing like my friend. The fact that I am not proves that he is a better person than I am.'

- Jane was envious of Beryl's ability to play the piano (object of envy: talent).

  Jane's unhealthy envy was both ego and non-ego in nature. She held the following irrational beliefs: 'Beryl must not be able to play the piano better than me. I can't bear the fact that I don't have her talent (non-ego) and because I don't this proves that she is worthier than me (ego).'

- Bill was envious of his friend's Porsche (object of envy: possession).

Bill's unhealthy envy was largely non-ego in nature. He held the following irrational beliefs: 'Bill must not have a Porsche when I don't have one. I can't bear the fact that he has what I don't have.'

Thinking that stems from unhealthy envy-based irrational beliefs

When a person holds an unhealthy envy-creating irrational belief, this belief will influence the way that she subsequently thinks.

Before I discuss these ways of thinking, let me stress an important point about unhealthy envy. At the heart of unhealthy envy is an intolerance of being in a disadvantaged position. Some instances of unhealthy envy are about making things equal. In one such case, the person is content (albeit for a short period) when she gets what she covets in the life of others. Here she is not concerned if others have it, as long as she has it. In the other case, if the person doesn't have whatever it is that she covets in the life of others, her object is to deprive them of what she covets, to spoil it for them or to destroy it. She is content (again albeit for a short period) that they don't have what she doesn't have.

Related to unhealthy envy (but not strictly speaking envy, since it does not involve the person being in a situation where she covets something belonging to someone else) is resentment about having to share what she covets. Here the person seeks to put herself in an advantaged position and the other in a disadvantaged position. She is not content to have what she covets if others have it too. She will only be content (in a disturbed sense) if she has it and others don't. Thus, she must get what she demands and make sure that others don't have it. Needless to say this is quite destructive and elements of this thinking are found in the thinking consequences of some unhealthy envy-related irrational beliefs.

Here are some common examples of such subsequent thinking.

Thinking obsessively about how to get what one envies regardless of its usefulness

When a person is unhealthily envious and she demands that she must get what the other person has that she lacks, she will find it easy to become obsessed with whatever it is that she covets, but does not have. Furthermore, she will think obsessively about getting it regardless of its usefulness to her and regardless of the price she may have to pay (financially and psychologically) in order to get it. In other words, such obsessive thinking flows fairly naturally from her unhealthy envy-based irrational beliefs.

Thinking about depriving the other person of what one envies

If the person's unhealthy envy-based irrational belief is centred on others not having what she doesn't have, she can strengthen this belief by thinking about what she can do to deprive the other person of what they have that she covets. She may picture herself taking whatever it is away from them and focus on the pleasure she experiences by so depriving them. As she does so, she may justify her actions by telling herself that she is righting a wrong. After all, she argues, it is dreadfully unfair if the other person has what she doesn't have and she is just making an unfair situation fair by depriving them of what she covets, but does not have.

On the other hand, if the person intends to keep whatever it is that she seeks to deprive them of, then she may tend to picture herself keeping it and she may justify her actions by showing herself how much she deserves to have whatever it is that she has coveted.

Thinking about spoiling or destroying what one envies so that the other doesn't have it

If the person can't deprive the other person of the object of her unhealthy envy, she can always make things equal in her mind by having thoughts and images of spoiling or destroying what the other has that she unhealthily covets. Again, as she fantasises about spoiling or destroying the other's possession, for example, she tends to focus on the pleasure that she will get from doing so and justifies her behaviour to herself accordingly.

Thinking obsessively of how to get what one covets and how to deprive, spoil or destroy the object of one's unhealthy envy for others

Here the person combines the thinking consequences discussed above. This cocktail is particularly potent in perpetuating her unhealthy envy-related irrational beliefs.

Thinking denigrating thoughts about the person who has what one envies

One way that the person can make things equal in her mind when she is feeling unhealthily envious is to denigrate in her mind the person who has what she envies. For example, Robert was unhealthily envious of furniture that his friends, Lisa and David, had. As a result he either told himself that they were greedy or that they were too ignorant to appreciate what they had. Thinking this way strengthened his conviction in his unhealthy envy-related beliefs and thus increased the probability that he would experience unhealthy envy in the future.

Thinking denigrating thoughts about the object of one's unhealthy envy

A similar equalising mental technique is for the person to denigrate in her mind the object of her unhealthy envy. This is the 'sour grapes' mentality. Thus, if a person covets the grapes that her friend has that she doesn't have, she can equalise this state of affairs for herself by thinking that the grapes are probably sour. This will help her to feel better momentarily, but to get worse in the longer term by strengthening her conviction in her unhealthy envy-based irrational belief and its distorted thinking conclusion: 'I must have what the other person has, and if I can't get it it's not worth having.'

Trying to convince oneself that one is happy with what one has and that one doesn't really desire what one envies

Another way of making things equal in the person's mind is to attempt to convince herself that she is happy with what she has and that she doesn't really want what she does, in reality, envy. Thus, if the person covets her friend's grapes (and holds unhealthy envy-related irrational beliefs about this situation), she will tend to make things equal in her mind by attempting to convince herself that the banana that she has is all that she really wants, when it isn't.

She can, of course, combine this strategy with the previous one and attempt to show herself: (a) that her banana is all that she really wants and (b) that her friend's grapes are, in all probability, sour.

Denying that one feels unhealthily envious

A number of the above thinking strategies involve the person lying to herself. This serves to perpetuate her unhealthy envy-related irrational beliefs in that she not only embellishes these beliefs, but she also protects them from investigation, and therefore change, by in effect denying that she feels unhealthily envious in the first place when in truth she does.

A stark and successful example of this is outright denial to herself that she does, in fact, feel unhealthily envious or that her envy is really healthy. An example of the former is to tell herself: 'No, I really don't want that' (when she really does) and an example of the latter is to tell herself: 'Yes, I would like that, but I don't need it' (when in reality she does believe that she really needs it). If the person can delude herself in these ways, this serves to keep her unhealthy envy-based irrational beliefs alive, making her vulnerable to unhealthy envy even though she will not admit to feeling it.

Behaviour that stems from unhealthy envy-based irrational beliefs

When a person holds unhealthy envy-based irrational beliefs, she will tend to act in certain ways. When she does act in these ways, she rehearses and therefore strengthens her conviction in these irrational beliefs.

Seeking out what one envies whether one really wants it or not

Once the person has identified the object of her unhealthy envy, she tends to devote a great deal of her time and effort pursuing it whether or not it is healthy for her to do so and whether or not it is really what she wants. Such striving will reinforce her unhealthy envy-based irrational beliefs.

Once one gets what one envies, one puts it to one side and focuses on something else to envy

If the person is successful in getting what she envies, she tends to put it to one side and looks around for something else that she covets that she doesn't have. When she finds it, she once again tends to pursue it in a very single-minded manner, while rehearsing her unhealthy envy-based irrational beliefs. She continues this pattern until it becomes second nature to her.

When she puts aside the object that she envied and obtained (after much striving), she reinforces the idea that what is essential to her is to get rid of the deprivation of not having what she thinks she must have rather than enjoying the envy object itself.

Other behaviour that stems from unhealthy envy-based irrational beliefs

The following involves the person putting into practice the thinking strategies discussed above. Thus, the person:

- Actively attempts to take away what she envies from the other.
- Actively attempts to spoil or destroy the envied object.
- Verbally disparages the person who has what she envies.
- Verbally disparages the envied object to others.
- Tells others that she doesn't really want what she envies.

It is important to appreciate that the person will rehearse her specific unhealthy envy-based irrational beliefs while carrying out these behaviours.

People develop and rehearse general unhealthy envy-based irrational beliefs

General unhealthy envy-based irrational beliefs are irrational beliefs that the person holds in many theme-related situations that enable her to experience unhealthy envy in these situations. If she develops and rehearses such beliefs, she will experience unhealthy envy in many different situations. She will do this mainly because she will become prone to focus on what she covets in the life of others that she doesn't have. Once she believes that she must have what she covets in the life of others, she will focus on what she doesn't have and edit out what she does have. Having identified a specific envy object in this way, she brings to it a specific variant of her general unhealthy envy-based irrational belief so that she makes herself unhealthily envious in this situation.

Having made herself feel unhealthily envious in this way, the person then tends to think and act in ways that are consistent with her unhealthy envy-based irrational beliefs and doing so strengthens her conviction in these beliefs. This increases the chance that she will perpetuate her unhealthy envy problem.

People develop and rehearse a view of the world founded on unhealthy envy-based irrational beliefs

For the last time, I want to stress that people develop world views that render them vulnerable to particular unhealthy negative emotions. The world views that render a person vulnerable to unhealthy envy do so because they make it very easy for her to focus on what she doesn't have (and covets) and to edit out in her mind what she does have. Then, as I have shown earlier in the chapter, the person makes herself unhealthily envious about this situation with the appropriate irrational beliefs. Here is an illustrative list of unhealthy envy-related world views that the person tends to develop and rehearse, and the inferences that they spawn.

World view: The grass is always greener in the lives of others.
Inference: Whatever I have is less attractive than what others have.

World view: Satisfaction can be achieved if only I get what I want.
Inference: If I get what I covet, it will satisfy me.
[This of course, is a delusion, since unhealthy envy-related irrational beliefs renders the person insatiable.]

World view: It's unfair if others have what I don't have, but it is fair if I have what others don't have.
Inference: If I don't have something that I covet that someone has, this inequality is unfair.

World view: People's worth is defined by what they have in life.
Inference: People will like me for what I have, rather than for who I am.

World view: The more I have, the happier I'll be.
Inference: In any situation, it is better to have what I don't have than to be content with what I do have.

Further reading

Academic

Salovey, P. (Ed.). (1991). *The psychology of jealousy and envy.* New York: Guilford.

Self-help

Dryden, W. (2002). *Overcoming envy.* London: Sheldon.

In the final chapter of the book, I will discuss how a person tends to maintain her emotional disturbance once she has created it. Before I do this though, let me present a summary of what I have discussed so far in this book. Figure 8.1 provides such a summary.

Emotion	Inference[1] in relation to personal domain[2]	Type of belief	Cognitive consequences	Action tendencies
Anxiety[3] (ego or discomfort)	• Threat or danger	Irrational	• Overestimates probability of threat occurring • Underestimates ability to cope with the threat • On reflection, creates an even more negative threat in one's mind • Has more task-irrelevant thoughts than in concern	• To withdraw physically from the threat • To withdraw mentally from the threat • To ward off the threat (e.g. by superstitious behaviour) • To tranquillise feelings • To seek reassurance
Depression[4] (ego or discomfort)	• Loss (with implications for future) • Failure	Irrational	• Sees only negative aspects of the loss or failure • Thinks of other losses and failures that one has experienced • Thinks one is unable to help self (helplessness) • Only sees pain and blackness in the future (hopelessness)	• To withdraw from reinforcements • To withdraw into oneself • To create an environment consistent with feelings • To attempt to terminate feelings of depression in self-destructive ways
Unhealthy anger	• Frustration • Goal obstruction • Self or other transgresses personal rule • Threat to self-esteem	Irrational	• Overestimates the extent to which the other person acted deliberately • Sees malicious intent in the motives of others • Self seen as definitely right; other(s) seen as definitely wrong • Unable to see the other person's point of view • Plots to exact revenge	• To attack the other physically • To attack the other verbally • To attack the other passive-aggressively • To displace the attack on to another person, animal or object • To withdraw aggressively • To recruit allies against the other

Emotion	Adversity		Thinking consequences	Behavioural consequences
Guilt	• Violation of moral code (sin of commission) • Failure to live up to moral code (sin of omission) • Hurts the feelings of a significant other	Irrational	• On reflection, assumes that one has definitely committed the sin • Assumes more personal responsibility than the situation warrants • Assigns far less responsibility to others than is warranted • Does not think of mitigating factors • Does not put behaviour into overall context • Thinks that one will receive retribution	• To escape from the unhealthy pain of guilt in self-defeating ways • To beg forgiveness from the person wronged • To promise unrealistically that one will not 'sin' again • To punish self physically or by deprivation • To disclaim responsibility for wrongdoing • To reject offers of forgiveness
Shame	• Something shameful has been revealed about self (or group with whom one identifies) by self or others • Acting in a way that falls very short of one's ideal • Others will look down on or shun self (or group with whom one identifies)	Irrational	• On reflection, overestimates the 'disgracefulness' of the information revealed • Overestimates the likelihood that the judging group will notice or be interested in the information • Overestimates the degree of disapproval self (or reference group) will receive • Overestimates the length of time any disapproval will last	• To remove self from the 'gaze' of others • To isolate self from others • To save face by attacking other(s) who have 'disgraced' self • To defend threatened self-esteem in self-defeating ways • To ignore attempts by others to restore social equilibrium

Figure 8.1 A diagrammatic summary of unhealthy negative emotions in REBT

Emotion	Inference[1] in relation to personal domain[2]	Type of belief	Cognitive consequences	Action tendencies
Hurt	• Other treats self badly (self undeserving)	Irrational	• Overestimates the unfairness of the other person's behaviour • Other perceived as showing lack of care or as indifferent • Self seen as alone, uncared for or misunderstood • Tends to think of past 'hurts' • Expects other to make the first move toward repairing relationship	• To shut down communication channel with the other • To sulk and make obvious one is hurt without disclosing details of the matter • To indirectly criticise or punish the other for the offence
Unhealthy jealousy	• Threat to relationship with partner from another person	Irrational	• Tends to see threats to one's relationship when none really exists • Thinks the loss of one's relationship is imminent • Misconstrues one's partner's ordinary conversations as having romantic or sexual connotations • Constructs visual images of partner's infidelity • If partner admits to finding another attractive, believes that the other is seen as more attractive than self and that one's partner will leave self for this other person	• To seek constant reassurance that one is loved • To monitor the actions, thoughts and feelings of one's partner • To search for evidence that one's partner is involved with someone else • To attempt to restrict the movements or activities of one's partner • To set tests that partner has to pass • To retaliate for partner's presumed infidelity • To sulk

		Irrational	
Unhealthy envy	• Another person possesses and enjoys something desirable that the person does not have	• Tends to denigrate the value of the desired possession and/or the person who possesses it • Tries to convince self that one is happy with one's possessions (although one is not) • Thinks about how to acquire the desired possession regardless of its usefulness • Thinks about how to deprive the other person of the desired possession • Thinks about how to spoil or destroy the 'other's' desired possession	• To disparage verbally the person who has the desired possession • To disparage verbally the desired possession • To take away the desired possession from the other (either so that one will have it or the other is deprived of it) • To spoil or destroy the desired possession so that the other person does not have it

Notes
1 Inference = Personally significant hunch that goes beyond observable reality and which gives meaning to it; may be accurate or inaccurate.
2 Personal domain = The objects – tangible and intangible – in which a person has an involvement (Beck, 1976)* REBT theory distinguishes between ego and comfort aspects of the personal domain, although those aspects frequently interact.
3 REBT theory distinguishes between ego anxiety and discomfort anxiety.
4 Depression in this context refers to non-clinical depression.

I wish to thank John Wiley & Sons Ltd for allowing me to use part of Figure 4.1 in Windy Dryden and Rhena Branch (2008) *The Fundamentals of Rational Emotive Behaviour Therapy: A Training Handbook* 2nd edition. Chichester: Wiley. Copyright John Wiley & Sons Ltd. Reproduced with permission.

* Beck, A.T. (1976) *Cognitive Therapy and the Emotional Disorders*. New York: International Universities Press.

Figure 8.1 (continued)

Chapter 9

How people maintain emotional problems

In each of the foregoing chapters I have taken a particular emotional problem, explained the REBT perspective on the emotion and how a person tends to, albeit unwittingly, perpetuate the problem. In this closing chapter, I will discuss, more generally, how people maintain their emotional problems.

Developing and practising a general philosophy of emotional disturbance

A person tends to maintain her emotional problems by developing and practising what I can best describe as a general philosophy of emotional disturbance. This philosophy comprises four irrational beliefs.

Demanding beliefs

When a person develops general demanding beliefs, she takes her preferences and turns these into absolute demands. A person is likely to have three main preferences:

- Preferences about self (e.g. 'I want to act morally'; 'I want to succeed').
- Preferences about others (e.g. 'I want you to approve of me'; 'I want you to be kind').
- Preferences about life conditions (e.g. 'I want life to be just').

The person then takes these desires and makes them rigid by turning them into absolute demands. Thus:

- Demands about self (e.g. 'I must act morally'; 'I must succeed').
- Demands about others (e.g. 'You must approve of me'; 'You must be kind').
- Demands about life conditions (e.g. 'Life must be just').

To create and maintain her emotional problems generally the person then applies these general demands to specific situations.

Awfulising beliefs

When a person develops general awfulising beliefs, she focuses generally on what she considers to be bad in life and then makes her evaluations extreme. She tells herself, for example 'It will be the end of the world if I don't succeed', 'It's terrible that you weren't kind' or 'It's awful if life is not just.' To create and maintain her emotional problems generally, the person then applies these general awfulising beliefs to specific situations whenever she encounters something that she considers bad in life.

Low frustration tolerance (LFT) beliefs

When a person develops general LFT beliefs she focuses generally on what she finds difficult to tolerate in life and then tells herself that she can't bear these conditions and that they not worth bearing, even though in reality they are.

Depreciation beliefs

A person can hold depreciation beliefs about herself, other people or life conditions. When a person develops depreciation beliefs she focuses generally on negative aspects about herself, another person or about life conditions and then gives herself, the other person or life conditions a global negative rating on the basis of that negative aspect. Thus:

- 'I am worthless for failing.'
- 'You are no good for treating people unkindly.'
- 'Life is no good for not giving me what I deserve.'

To create and maintain her emotional problems generally the person then applies these general depreciation beliefs to specific situations whenever she encounters negative aspects of self, others and life.

The person then maintains her emotional problems generally by thinking and acting in ways that are consistent with the four irrational beliefs that comprise this philosophy. I have given many different examples of how people tend to do this in the previous chapters.

Denying that one has emotional problems

Once a person has made disturbance in herself, she maintains this disturbance by denying to herself that she has a problem. If the person does this successfully, it means that, since she does not acknowledge that she feels feel disturbed, then she does not need to do anything constructive about it. Doing nothing constructive about emotional disturbance will lead to its perpetuation.

Even if the person admits to having a problem, she tends to maintain this problem by denying to others that she has a problem. Doing so means that the person deprives herself of potential help for her problem, which she will then unwittingly maintain when she does not know how to help herself.

Not taking responsibility for one's emotional problems

Just because a person admits to having an emotional problem, it does not follow that she will take responsibility for it. There are a number of ways in which a person can refrain from taking such responsibility. Here are some examples:

- Blaming one's parents (e.g. 'My parents have made me anxious and insecure').
- Blaming one's genes (e.g. 'I'm a born worrier. Always have been, always will be. It's in my genes').
- Blaming one's past environment (e.g. 'I grew up in a family in which nobody expressed how they felt. That's why I'm scared of conflict today').
- Blaming one's present environment (e.g. 'The uncertainty at work causes my panic').

- Blaming past experiences (e.g. 'I was bullied at school. That caused me to be scared of people').
- Blaming present experiences (e.g. 'Being made redundant has made me depressed').

There is an element of truth to all these statements in that all the above-mentioned factors do *contribute* to a person's current emotional disturbance. However, in reality, they do not *cause* her disturbed feelings, which are largely determined by her irrational beliefs about events as outlined throughout this book.

Refraining from taking responsibility for her emotional problems means that the person will not do anything to change them, which, in effect, means that she will maintain them.

Disturbing oneself about one's emotional problems

Once a person makes herself emotionally disturbed, then she can perpetuate this problem by disturbing herself about it. Not only does this maintain this first problem (for how can the person address this problem effectively when she is disturbing herself about it?), the person gives herself a second emotional problem: two problems for the price of one, as it were.

There are two major ways that a person gives herself a meta-emotional problem (an emotional problem about an emotional problem). First, she can do this in the ego domain (e.g. 'I must not get myself unhealthily angry and if I do this proves that I am an inadequate person') and second, she can do so in the non-ego domain (e.g. 'I must not get myself unhealthily angry. I can't bear the experience of feeling unhealthily angry').

Here are examples of common meta-emotional problems:

- Anxiety about anxiety (e.g. 'I must not feel anxious and if I do, it would be unbearable').
- Shame about unhealthy envy (e.g. 'I must not show that I am unhealthily envious and if I do, it proves that I am a disgusting person').
- Guilt about the expression of unhealthy anger (e.g. 'I must not show my unhealthy anger and if I do, it proves that I am a bad person').

- Depression about depression (e.g. 'I must not make myself depressed and if I do, it proves that I am a weak, inadequate person).
- Anxiety about hurt (e.g. 'I must not feel hurt and if I do, I won't be able to stand it').

Seeking out the payoffs of having emotional problems

A person can maintain her emotional problems by focusing on and seeking out payoffs that stem from being emotionally disturbed. Here are some representative examples of such payoffs.

Payoffs for being emotionally disturbed

- A person may get sympathy from other people.
- People may help her out with a variety of tasks.
- She can get time off from work and still get paid.
- She may get early retirement on health grounds and get her pension paid early.
- People may be reluctant to ask her to do difficult tasks.
- People will tend not to put the person under stress so that she gets an easier life.
- People will be less likely to have high expectations of the person.
- She may be able to get people to do what she wants them to do by reminding them verbally or by her actions that she suffers from emotional disturbance.
- Some people will look after her.
- If the person is a student, she may be able to get her degree without doing any work by dint of being emotionally disturbed (such a degree is called an aegrotat).
- If the person fails at anything, then she can attribute this failure to the fact that she was emotionally disturbed ('It wasn't me, it was my illness').

Avoiding the costs of being psychologically healthy

A person can also maintain her emotional problems by not addressing her problem constructively, thus avoiding the costs of being psychologically healthy. Here are some representative examples of such costs.

Costs of being psychologically healthy

- People may expect much of the person and may well be disappointed in her if she fails to live up to their expectations.
- She may be expected to carry the workload of others who are off sick (including those who are away from work due to psychological problems!).
- People may ask her to do onerous tasks because they think she is healthy enough to cope with them.
- She will get little sympathy from people if she shows how emotionally healthy she is.
- People may expect her to look after them. They will certainly not want to look after her.
- Few people will offer to help her with things.
- If she fails at anything she will not have anything or anyone to attribute this failure to, only herself.
- People will probably not make allowances for her.

Making and acting on self-fulfilling prophecies

People often maintain their emotional problems by constructing and acting on self-fulfilling prophecies. Here is an example of a self-fulfilling prophecy. Jack made himself disturbed by developing and rehearsing the following irrational belief: 'I must do well socially and I am an inadequate person if I don't.' This irrational belief produced the following unhealthy consequences for Jack:

- Emotional consequences: anxiety; shame.
- Behavioural consequences: avoidance of social situations; withdrawal from social situations.
- Thinking consequences: 'Nobody will want to talk to me if I go out'; 'If people talk to me they will think that I am strange'.

Jack was invited to a party and he was unable to get out of going. Jack took the following steps that constituted the development and implementation of a self-fulfilling prophecy.

1   Jack took one of his thinking consequences and tailored it to the specific situation he was about to face (e.g. 'When I go to the party nobody will talk to me').

2   He acted in a way to bring about this result. (He did not talk to anyone and made it difficult for anybody to talk to him. He avoided all eye contact and didn't reply or grunted if anyone tried to talk to him.)

3   When he achieved this result, Jack used it to justify the accuracy of his original prediction and as evidence for the accuracy of his irrational belief (e.g. 'You see, I was right all along. I went to the party and nobody spoke to me. This proves that I am an inadequate person').

4   He didn't take any responsibility for bringing about the result that he predicted (i.e. he did not acknowledge that his behaviour actively discouraged people from talking to him).

Developing blocks to personal change

People tend to develop a range of reasons why they can't or won't change. The following is a list of commonly encountered blocks:

- 'I'm too old to change.'
- 'I'm too set in my ways to change.'
- 'I have held my irrational beliefs for too long to change them now.'
- 'Personal change is too hard.'
- 'Personal change will be too disruptive to my life.'
- 'I'm too lazy to change.'
- 'I fail at everything that I do, so there's no point me trying to change since I'm bound to fail.'
- 'Other people need to change, I don't.'
- 'It's unfair that I suffer from emotional disturbance when others don't. I shouldn't therefore have to work hard to change myself.'
- 'I'm used to who I am. If I change, I wouldn't know who I am.'
- 'My past has irrevocably damaged me. So change is not possible.'
- 'My emotional disturbance is inherited, so I can't do anything to help myself since my problems are in my genes.'

The impact of such blocks is that they stop the person from even testing them out, since they are hypotheses about change rather than fact. As the person treats them as incontrovertible facts, she refrains from doing anything sustained to help herself address her emotional problems effectively, thus perpetuating them.

Complaining endlessly to people about one's emotional problems and using the 'yes–but' technique when given encouragement and helpful advice

Another way that a person resists personal change and thus unwittingly maintains her emotional problems is by complaining endlessly about things she disturbs herself about and by negating any constructive help and encouragement she may get from others. Here the person employs the famous yes–but technique popularised by Eric Berne (1964) in his book *Games People Play*. When a person uses this technique, she seems to agree with another person's advice or she seems to respond constructively to their encouragement (i.e. 'yes. . . . . .'), and then explains why she can't take the advice or why the encouragement is misplaced (i.e. 'but. . . . . .').

Here is an illustrative dialogue to demonstrate how a person can perpetuate her emotional disturbance by complaining and resisting change using the 'yes–but' technique.

Beryl: I'm too scared to apply for that job that you told me about.

Friend: You've got no reason to be scared, you could do that job blind-folded.

Beryl: That's kind of you to say so, but technology has moved on a lot since I last worked in the field.

Friend: But you are bright and you could easily update yourself on those developments.

Beryl: Yes that may have been the case once, but I've lost my confidence.

Friend: Your confidence will come back if you take the risk and do things unconfidently for a while.

Beryl: Yes that would have probably been the case when I was younger, but now I'm older I can't do that.

Friend: Wow, you are really down on yourself. I suggest that you see a counsellor.

Beryl: Yes, that's a good idea, but I can't afford to.

Friend: I'll lend you the money.

Beryl: That's very kind of you, but I hate borrowing money from anyone.

Friend: OK. I'll pay for the counselling.

Beryl: That's enormously kind of you, but that will put me under too much pressure to change and I really feel that I can't change.

An undesired consequence of using the complaining 'yes–but' combination is that the person will eventually alienate her friends. If this happens, the person may well complain about it to others and eventually alienate them by consistent application of the 'yes–but' technique.

Developing doubts, reservations and objections to a philosophy of psychological health

The final way that a person maintains her emotional problems that I want to discuss involves her taking the healthy alternative to her general disturbance-creating philosophy that I discussed at the beginning of this chapter and constructing a number of doubts, reservations and objections to what might be called a philosophy of psychological health. Before I discuss such doubts, reservations and objections, let me briefly outline the four rational beliefs that comprise this healthy philosophy.

Non-dogmatic or full preference beliefs

In order to implement what I call non-dogmatic or full preference beliefs, the person asserts what she wants (partial preferences) and negates the demand that she has to get what she wants. A person has three partial preferences:

- Partial preferences about self (e.g. 'I want to act morally'; 'I want to succeed').
- Partial preferences about others (e.g. 'I want you to be kind').

- Partial preferences about life conditions (e.g. 'I want life to be just').

Then, taking these partial preferences, the person keeps them flexible by refraining from turning them into absolute demands. These are known as non-dogmatic or full preferences. Thus:

- Non-dogmatic or full preferences about self (e.g. 'I want to act morally, but I don't have to do so'; 'I want to succeed, but I don't have to do so').
- Non-dogmatic or full preferences about others (e.g. 'I want you to be kind, but there is no reason why you have to be kind').
- Non-dogmatic or full preferences about life conditions (e.g. 'I want life to be just, but it doesn't have to be just').

Anti-awfulising beliefs

In order to implement anti-awfulising beliefs, the person focuses generally on what she considers to be bad in life and then negates the extreme evaluations that I discussed under awfulising beliefs earlier in this book. Thus:

- 'It will be bad if I don't succeed, but it wouldn't be the end of the world.'
- 'It's unfortunate that you weren't kind, but it's not terrible.'
- 'It's bad if life is not just, but it is not awful.'

High frustration tolerance (HFT) beliefs

In order to implement HFT beliefs, the person needs to focus on what she finds difficult to tolerate in life and then tell herself that she can bear it and that it is worth bearing. Thus:

- 'It would be hard to put up with not succeeding, but it's tolerable and worth tolerating.'
- 'It's a struggle bearing you not being kind, but it's bearable and worth bearing.'
- 'It's difficult to stand it if life is not just, but I can stand it and it is worth it to me to do so.'

Acceptance beliefs

A person can hold acceptance beliefs about herself, other people or life conditions. In order to implement acceptance beliefs, the person focuses on something negative about herself, another person or about life conditions and then refrains from giving herself, the other person or life conditions a global negative rating on the basis of that negative aspect. Rather, she shows herself that she and the other person are complex, fallible human beings comprising many good, bad and neutral aspects, who can legitimately rate such aspects of themselves but cannot legitimately give themselves a global rating. Similarly, she shows herself that life conditions are made up of many good, bad and neutral features and cannot legitimately be given a global rating.

Thus:

- 'I am not worthless for failing. I am a fallible human being who has failed this time, but who is capable of achieving success and failure.'
- 'You are a fallible human being and are not worthless for treating people unkindly, but you have acted badly when you treat people in this way.'
- 'When life does not give me what I deserve it is bad in this respect, but it is not bad in its entirety. Life is a complex mixture of good, bad and neutral features.'

Now, when the person has doubts, reservations and objections to these rational beliefs and these doubts etc. are not addressed, she will resist acquiring the rational belief and maintain her emotional problems as a consequence.

Here are a few examples of people's doubts, reservations and objections to rational beliefs:

- Adopting non-dogmatic or full preferences means losing my motivation. Demands are motivating.
- Adopting non-dogmatic or full preferences means adopting a 'don't care' attitude. Demands prove that I care.
- Some things really are awful. Adopting anti-awfulising beliefs means that I am persuading myself that what is awful really isn't.

- Adopting anti-awfulising beliefs means I am condoning bad things.
- Adopting HFT beliefs means that I will put up with being treated badly.
- Adopting HFT beliefs means lying to myself that I can stand what I really can't, since many things in life are truly intolerable.
- Adopting self-acceptance beliefs means that I resign myself to being who I am.
- Adopting other-acceptance beliefs means condoning the very bad things that people do to one another.

All of these are misconceptions as I have discussed elsewhere (Dryden, 2001), but when left unchallenged they do serve to maintain emotional disturbance.

This is now the end of the book. I hope you have found it useful and would appreciate any feedback c/o the publisher.

Reference

Dryden, W. (2001). *Reason to change: A rational emotive behaviour therapy (REBT) workbook*. Hove, UK: Routledge.

Index

unhealthy envy: and behavioural effects of irrational beliefs 118–19, 125; ego and non-ego 112–15; healthy envy and 110; inferences related to 111–15, 120; irrational beliefs based on 112–20; shame about 129; and thinking effects of irrational beliefs 115–18, 125; world views and unhealthy envy-based irrational beliefs 120

unhealthy jealousy: and behavioural effects of irrational beliefs 103–7, 124; healthy jealousy and 97; inferences related to 98–100, 106–9; irrational beliefs based on 99–109; suspicion and 101, 103–5; and thinking effects of

irrational beliefs 101–3, 124; world views and unhealthy jealousy-based irrational beliefs 108–9

verbal attack 80, 122; verbal disparagement 119

withdrawal 48–50, 122; aggressive 82; sulking 93–4, 124

world views: anxiety and 18–19; depression and 36; guilt and 68–9; hurt and 95; shame and 51–2; unhealthy anger and 83–4; unhealthy envy and 120; unhealthy jealousy and 108–9

'yes–but' technique 133–4

Printed in Great Britain
by Amazon